F-15 Eagle 104, MiGs Nil

Introduced as a McDonnell Douglas jet in the early 1970s, the F-15 Eagle remains the world's greatest post-war fighter. To quote F-15 pilot, Colonel Cesar Rodriguez: "Many may not know it, but the F-15 air-to-air victory scorecard of 104 to zero has no peer in the modern era of next generation fighters." Accounts of the F-15 as given by Colonel Rodriguez can be found in MiG Killer on pages 30 to 39.

Dubbed the 'Tennis Court' because of its extensive top side, the F-15 is a big, powerful, and lethal killing machine. F-15 pilots love flying the jet to such an extent that many, without complacency, feel more confidence in being able to defeat an adversary. Its weapons remain both effective and lethal, today the F-15 is armed with AIM-9 Sidewinder and AIM-120 AMRAAM missiles and the M61A1 20mm Vulcan gatling gun. Of yesterday, the Eagle's big stick was the AIM-7 Sparrow missile which scalped 24 Iraqi aircraft and helicopters in Operation Desert Storm back in 1991.

In the late 1970s, a US Air Force requirement for a tactical strike aircraft resulted in the F-15E Strike Eagle. Designed as a multi-role aircraft, like its F-15 Eagle sister ship, the F-15E is also proven in combat, and remains the US Air Force's tactical strike aircraft of choice, one with a lethal air-to-air capability and bucketloads of performance.

This special publication provides accounts of the experiences of pilots and maintainers who operated the F-15 in peacetime, on alert and in combat. Whether you're an avid aviation enthusiast or somebody with a particular interest in great fighter aircraft, *F-15 Eagle* is an essential read.

Mark Ayton
Editor

US Air Force/Senior Airman Christopher Sparks

CONTENTS

US Air National Guard/ Lieutenant Colonel Bill Ramsay

US Air Force/TSgt John Raven

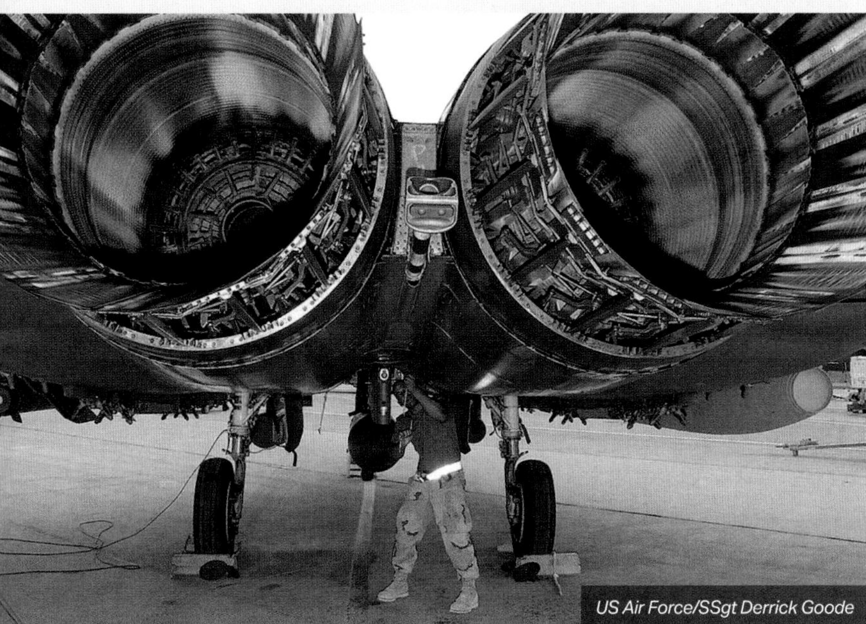
US Air Force/SSgt Derrick Goode

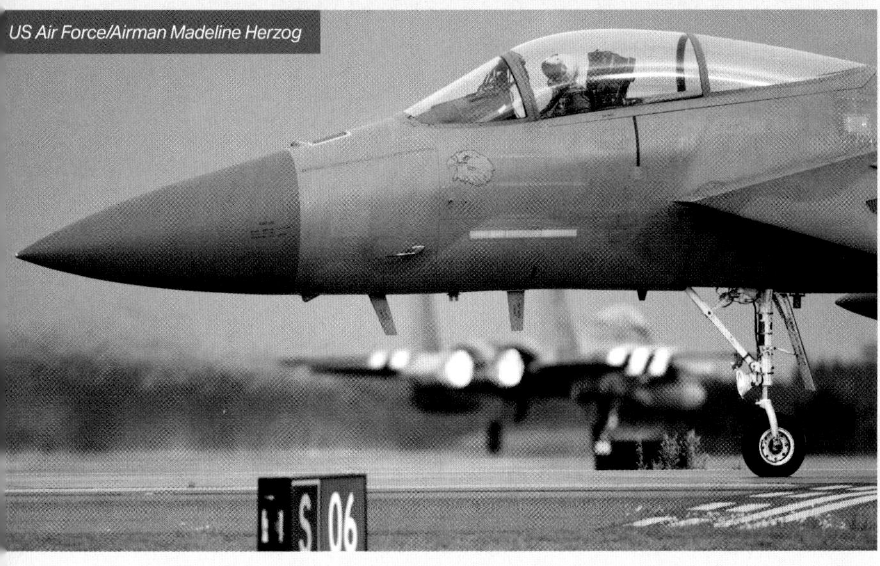

US Air Force/Airman Madeline Herzog

ISBN: 978 1 80282 987 7
Editor: Mark Ayton
Senior editor, specials: Roger Mortimer
Email: roger.mortimer@keypublishing.com
Cover Design: Steve Donovan
Design: SJmagic DESIGN SERVICES, India
Advertising Sales Manager: Sam Clark
Email: sam.clark@keypublishing.com
Tel: 01780 755131
Advertising Production: Becky Antoniades
Email: Rebecca.antoniades@keypublishing.com

SUBSCRIPTION/MAIL ORDER
Key Publishing Ltd, PO Box 300, Stamford, Lincs, PE9 1NA
Tel: 01780 480404
Subscriptions email: subs@keypublishing.com
Mail Order email: orders@keypublishing.com
Website: www.keypublishing.com/shop

PUBLISHING
Group CEO and Publisher: Adrian Cox

Published by
Key Publishing Ltd, PO Box 100, Stamford, Lincs, PE9 1XQ
Tel: 01780 755131
Website: www.keypublishing.com

PRINTING
Precision Colour Printing Ltd, Haldane, Halesfield 1, Telford, Shropshire. TF7 4QQ

DISTRIBUTION
Seymour Distribution Ltd, 2 Poultry Avenue, London, EC1A 9PU
Enquiries Line: 02074 294000.

KEY Publishing

Origins of the F-15 Eagle

To appreciate the F-15 it is important to understand the conception of the aircraft. This chapter comprises directly quoted excerpts from Jacob Neufeld's official, now declassified, F-15 Eagle Origins and Development publication of November 1974.

F-15A 71-0280 during its first flight on July 27, 1972, piloted by McDonnell-Douglas' chief test pilot Irving Burrows. The 50-minute maiden flight was flown from Edwards US Air Force Base, California. US Air Force

In June 1965, Tactical Air Command (TAC) convened a select panel of field commanders to consider the projected Soviet tactical fighter threat. In a departure from concepts pursued in USAF tactical fighter development over recent years, the panel expressed a clear preference for a lightweight day fighter. Their model was a single-seat, twin-engine aircraft in the 20,000 to 25,000-pound class. Though asking for an aircraft that could fly from Mach . 2 on the deck up to Mach 2.5, the panel tressed manoeuvrability more than speed. 'he panel's report was not distributed; owever, its conclusions served as a kind of ramework for the TAC position.

On August 1, 1965, General Gabriel)isosway - a World War Two fighter ilot commander - took over TAC and nmediately reviewed the work undertaken y Colonel John Burns, Assistant Director f Requirements, Headquarters, Tactical Air Command (TAC) and wasted little time in ssuing Qualitative Operation Requirement QOR) 65-14-F on October 6. The document, ent to the Air Staff, emphasized TAC's nterest in an 'aircraft capable of out-erforming the enemy in the air.'

Besides challenging the notion that only a nulti-purpose fighter could gain Office of the Secretary of Defense (OSD) and Congressional pproval and bringing the controversy into he open, it specified an aircraft like the one lescribed by the June 1965 TAC panel, xcept that it raised the plane's weight to a 0,000-35,000-pound range. The requirement lso called for providing the new aircraft with radar capability similar to the F-4's and that be equipped with both infrared and radar nissiles. TAC also emphasized the need for nanoeuvring performance and high thrustto-weight ratio but for temperature limitation, it lowered the maximum speed requirement from Mach 3.0 to Mach 2.5 - a change that would save between 35 and 40 percent of the total cost, or $4.5 versus $2.5 million per copy.

THE PIVOTAL DECISION

In July, Secretary McNamara endorsed the US Air Force's prerequisite work on developing a new F-X fighter.

F-X work statements were revised to call for an aircraft with the 'best combination of air-to-air and air-to-ground characteristics' vis-à-vis the previous description of the development as aiming at medium-cost, multi-purpose aircraft, highlighting close air support. Although this change seemed mere semantics, it permitted the US Air Force to launch a major effort to acquire a new fighter.

General Disosway and his operations advisors, Colonels Burns and Gordon Graham, believed that air superiority was essential throughout the spectrum of tactical warfare. Given the limitations on the employment of tactical air power, such as the enemy sanctuaries that existed during the Korean and Vietnam Wars, an uncompromised fighter was needed to sweep the skies clear of enemy aircraft. They argued that the only way the US Air Force could meet the challenge posed by lightweight, manoeuvrable Soviet fighters in the 1970s was to design a superior air combat fighter.

Lieutenant General James Ferguson, Deputy Chief of Staff for R&D, who became commander of the US Air Force Systems Command (AFSC) in September 1966, asked General Disoway to await the results of parametric design studies that began in March 1966. Ferguson personally opposed the parametric study requirement but believed the results would substantiate the case for an air superiority fighter. Six types of aircraft. including two 'families' of low, medium, and high-cost fighters (costing $1.8, $2.5, and $3.2 million respectively) were studied. One family of fighters studied emphasized air combat capability with ground attack being a secondary requirement. whereas the second examined the effect of reversing the mission order.

ENERGY MANOEUVRABILITY

General Ferguson and his development planners, Major General Glenn Kent, and Brigadier General F. M. Rogers, sensed that the F-X requirements were 'badly spelled out.' They subsequently were able to persuade General Disoway to modify his requirements, thanks in large part to the work of Major John Boyd. In October 1966 Boyd joined the Tactical Division of the Air Staff Directorate of Requirements. When asked to comment on the 'Representative F-X design,' he summarily rejected it. A veteran pilot of the late 1950s and author of the air combat training manual used by the Fighter Weapons School at Nellis US Air Force Base, Nevada, Boyd was well qualified to assess fighter aircraft. In 1962, while completing an engineering course at Georgia Tech, he studied the relationships between energy and energy changes of aircraft during flight and devised a method to measure aircraft manoeuvrability - the ability to change altitude, airspeed, and direction.

Major Boyd continued his energy manoeuvrability (EM) studies at his next station, Eglin Air Force Base, Florida, even though his primary assignment there was maintenance officer. At Eglin he met Thomas Christie, a mathematician who also saw promise in the EM theory and who had access to a large-capacity, high-speed computer. With Christie's help Major Boyd gained access

The F-15 made its ceremonial debut at McDonnell-Douglas' St Louis plant on June 26, 1972. Appropriately painted in air superiority blue and christened the Eagle, it was hailed as America's first air superiority fighter since the F-86 appeared some 20 years earlier. *Boeing/McDonnell-Douglas*

to the computer to confirm his calculations. For this irregularity - i.e., working outside authorized channels - they were both severely criticized. However, with the help of Brigadier General Allman Culbertson, Air Proving Ground Center (APGC) vice commander, Boyd and Christie fought off repeated attempts to terminate their studies and in May 1964 published an official two-volume treatise on energy manoeuvrability.

Working within the Tactical Division, Major Boyd began to apply the EM theory to the F-X, projecting how the aircraft would perform in the critical manoeuvring performance envelope - the subsonic and transonic speeds up to Mach 1.6 and altitudes up to 30,000 feet. He then asked TAC, ASD, and the study contractors to provide trade-offs between range, structural requirements, and on-board equipment. Then, by comparing configuration changes for fixed and variable wing sweeps, Major Boyd designed a model that would demonstrate the effects of specific requirements on the F-X design. For example, he could show the manoeuvrability penalty that TAC would have to pay if it desired the F-X to have a given range.

By the spring of 1967, through the efforts of Boyd and others, a 40,000-pound F-X aircraft was 'popped out.' Its proposed engine bypass had been lowered to 1.5, thrust-to-weight increased to 0.97 and the F-X top speed scaled down to a range of Mach 2.3 to 2.5. During the various design trade-offs, Major Boyd challenged the validity of ASD's drag polars (lift versus drag charts) and argued that lower wing loadings on the order of 80 pounds/square feet would be more appropriate for the F-X design.

Doggedly pursuing his research into drag polars, he later examined the effects of optimizing propulsion, configuration, avionics, and weapons for the fixed and variable sweep-wing designs. His calculations of these trade-offs pointed to 0.6 as the 'best' engine bypass ratio and to a 60 to 65 pounds/square feet wing loading. The design studies incorporated into the final F-15 configuration confirmed these values.

CONCEPT FORMULATION

The F-X formulation phase continued through the spring and summer of 1967. By March, a three-part Concept Formulation Package (CFP) and a Technical Development Plan (TDP) were drafted to specify the F-X rationale, cost, and development schedule. In June, a complete CFP was issued and underwent a final Air Staff-ANSER 'massaging' by August 1967. Secretary Brown then submitted the revised cost proposal to OSD as the US Air Force's recommended new tactical fighter candidate to replace the F-4. He noted the US Air Force's tactical force structure for the mid-1970s limited to 24 wings by OSD - included 13 F-4, six F-111 and five A-7 wings that were respectively oriented to perform counter air interdiction, and close air support missions. Secretary Brown now argued for the paramountcy of counterair (air superiority), without which the other missions would be either too costly or impossible, and the need to protect ground forces against enemy air attack.

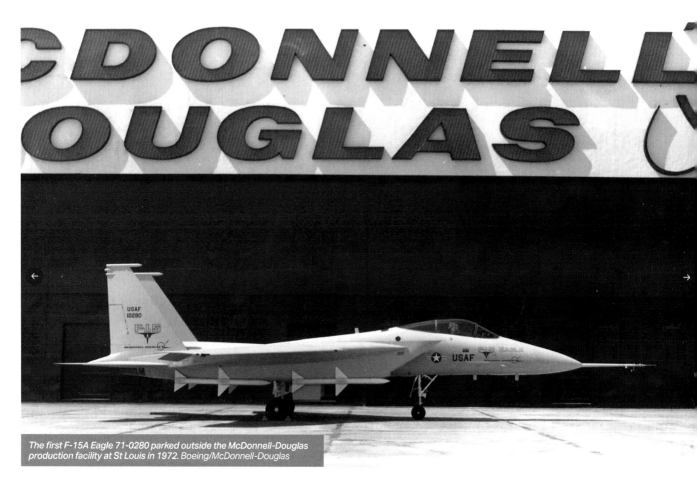

The first F-15A Eagle 71-0280 parked outside the McDonnell-Douglas production facility at St Louis in 1972. Boeing/McDonnell-Douglas

He noted that although the multi-purpose F-4 Vietnam workhorse was a capable air-to-air fighter, its continued effectiveness was doubtful in view of the appearance of a new, advanced Soviet fighter series. US intelligence projected that by the mid-1970s approximately half the Soviet tactical aircraft inventory would consist of such modern fighters as the *Fitter* (Su-7) and Twin Sukhoi (68-TF), both said to excel the F-4 in air combat.

The US Air Force Secretary noted that recent Soviet fighter designs concentrated on improving range and payload. US tactical air superiority in the Korean and Vietnam Wars was attributed to 'superior pilot skill and better armament and avionics.' These advantages were not expected to prevail in a conventional war in Europe, for example, because of the likelihood of encountering well-trained Soviet pilots. Moreover, the Soviets were increasing their manoeuvrability edge and significantly improving their missile and fire-control systems. The US Air Force cautioned that it could no longer 'rely on pilot skill alone to offset any technical inferiority of US aircraft.... To win an air war against Soviet forces it is essential that US pilots be given the best aircraft that technology can afford.'

The various US Air Force analyses, Secretary Brown said, indicated that little improvement could be expected from modifying existing aircraft such as the F-4, F-111. YF-12, A-7, and a US-German V /STOL design. Additionally, the cost of such an effort would be extremely high, approaching that required to develop a completely new fighter. It conceded that additional study was requirec to refine the F-X characteristics, but tentativel recommended a 'representative' fighter as "a 40,000-pound single-place fighter with a variable sweep wing, powered by two high-thrust turbofan engines... capable of sustainec flight at Mach 2.3 with a burst capability to Mach 2.5. The avionics... [included] advanced dual mode radar, internally carried penetration aids, and advanced navigation, communications, computation, and identification equipment. The F-X armament will consist of long-range radar missiles, short range IR or electrooptical missiles, and an internal gun. [In addition, it] would be equippec to deliver with improved accuracy, all the ballistic air-to-ground munitions and air-to-ground guided missiles in the USAF tactical inventory during the period 1970 to 1980."

Total F-X costs were estimated at $7.183 billion, including $615 million for R&D, $4.1 billion for procurement, and $2.468 billion for operations and maintenance over a five-year span. Based on a 1,000 aircraft buy, the averag F-X flyaway cost was computed at $2.84 millior per copy. The proposed initial operational capability (IOC) date was December 1973.

In his memorandum to Mr McNamara, Secretary Brown reiterated that there were several unresolved areas involving the 'Representative F-X,' such as whether or not the proposed aircraft could be flown by a single pilot. He said that additional wind-tunnel testing was required to confirm the effectiveness of certain high-lift devices and more detailed work was needed to define the F-X engines and avionics. Dr Brown also foreshadowed the commonality issue by predicting that certain components and

This photo of F-15A 71-0280 during an early test flight from Edwards US Air Force Base shows the full extent of the high-visibility dayglo colour applied to different surfaces on the aircraft. During the F-15's flight test programme, this aircraft was used to explore the flight envelope, general handling, and carriage of external stores. US Air Force

F-15 EAGLE DEVELOPMENT TEST FLEET

Serial number	Model	First Flight	Location of first flight	Test activities
71-0280	F-15A	June 26, 1972	KEDW	Flight envelope, general handling, and external stores carriage.
71-0281	F-15A	September 26, 1972	KSTL	F100 engine.
71-0282	F-15A	November 4, 1972	KSTL	Radar, avionics, and air speed.
71-0283	F-15A	January 13, 1973	KSTL	Structural test bed.
71-0284	F-15A	March 7, 1973	KSTL	Weapons and external stores.
71-0285	F-15A	May 23, 1973	KSTL	Avionics and fire control system.
71-0286	F-15A	June 14, 1973	KSTL	Weapons and external stores.
71-0287	F-15A	August 25, 1973	KSTL	Spin recovery, angle-of-attack, and fuel system.
71-0288	F-15A	October 20, 1973	KSTL	Aircraft and engine integration.
71-0289	F-15A	January 16, 1974	KSTL	Radar, avionics, and electronic warfare systems.
71-0290	F-15B, built as a TF-15A	July 7, 1973	KSTL	Flight envelope, general handling.
71-0291	F-15B, built as a TF-15A	October 18, 1973	KSTL	Conformal fuel tanks.

Key
KEDW denotes Edwards Air Force Base, California
KSTL denotes St Louis-Lambert Field, Missouri

subsystems of the F-X and the Navy's VFAX could be made interchangeable. He was less optimistic regarding "the extent to which common airframe assemblies may be used for these two aircraft."

POINT DESIGN STUDIES

On August 11, 1967, the US Air Force solicited bids from seven aerospace companies for a second round of studies. These 'point design' studies sought to refine the F-X concept in four areas: (1) validating the aircraft's performance in wind tunnel tests; (2) matching propulsion requirements against performance; (3) examining the preferred avionics and armaments systems; and (4) studying the effects of crew size. In short, the effort was to establish a technical base for the F-X proposal. On December 1, the US Air Force awarded study contracts to General Dynamics and McDonnell-Douglas, while Fairchild-Hiller, Grumman, Lockheed, and North American undertook unfunded studies. All investigations were completed by June 1968, at which time a composite US Air Force team assembled at Wright-Patterson US Air Force Base, Ohio, to 'scrub down' the results and rewrite the Concept Formulation Package.

More than 100 people helped in the scrub down effort headed by Colonel Robert Daly. The basic airframe issues were resolved within reasonable time, but the avionics caused considerable disagreement. A major issue in the avionics controversy concerned the F-X fire control system. Specifically, the multi-purpose advocates tried to retain such items as terrain-following radar and blind-bombing capability. They argued that 'advances' in radar, antennas, and computers would permit inclusion of these features, but overlooked both the costs and risks involved. The scrub down was only partly successful, since many high-risk, high-cost items remained.

CONCEPT FORMULATION PACKAGE SUPPLEMENT

Although differences remained, the point design-studies and scrub down proved fruitful. In August 1968, the Air Staff issued a supplement to the Concept Formulation Package (CFP) that not only updated the original formulation document but also recommended some fundamental changes. For example, there no longer remained any ambivalence over the US Air Force's air superiority doctrine. Thus. the CFP supplement stated: "It is sometimes held that air combat of the future will assume an entirely different complexion than that of the past. The US Air Force does not share that contention. To the contrary, tactical applications of air superiority forces will remain essentially the same for the foreseeable future."

It further noted that the war in Southeast Asia had taught the US Air Force that smaller-sized aircraft could better escape radar and visual detection. Thus, the supplement specified a one-man crew for the F-X but retained a two-man trainer version. The wing planform remained open, although the 'Representative F-X' described a swing-wing rather than a fixed-wing design. The major subsystems - engine, radar, and cannon - would be selected on a competitive flyoff basis. While the US Air Force did not resolve some of the difficult issues, it decided to stress the air superiority aspects of the F-X and relegated to a secondary or bonus status air-to-ground capabilities.

F-X costs in the August 1968 CFP supplement were presented on a different basis than they had been the previous year. In 1967, for example, cost estimates were predicted on a 10-year, 1,000 aircraft buy, whereas the 1968 estimates considered a 635-aircraft production run.

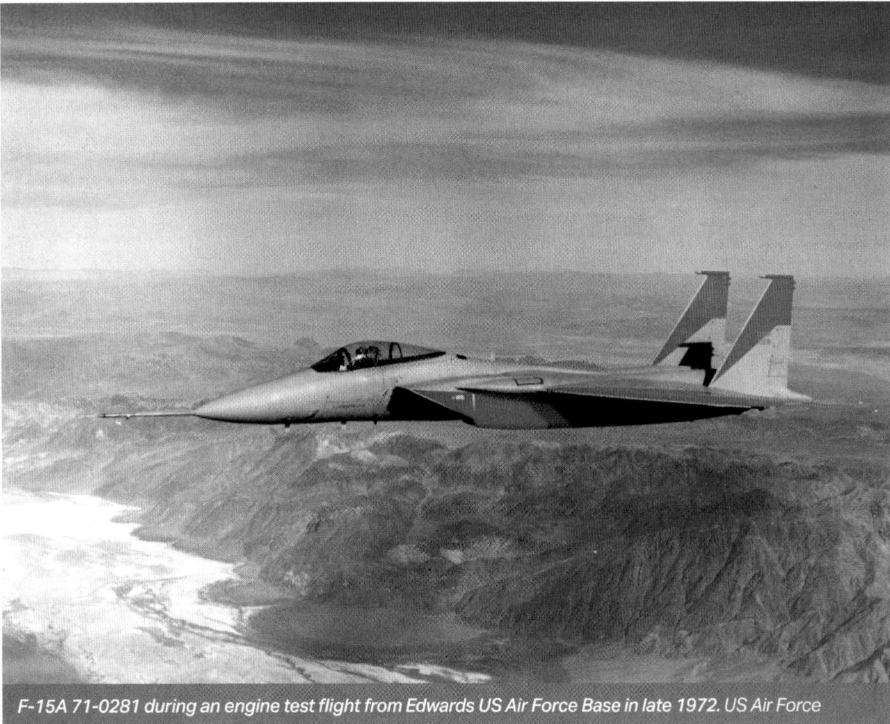

F-15A 71-0281 during an engine test flight from Edwards US Air Force Base in late 1972. US Air Force

On August 15, General John McConnell, Chief of Staff of the US Air Force approved the F-X source selection plans and the joint US Air Force-Navy engine development program. Secretary Brown's endorsement came the next month.

CONTRACT DEFINITION

On September 30, 1968, the US Air Force launched the F-X contract definition phase by soliciting bids from eight aircraft companies. Only four contractors responded - Fairchild-Hiller, General Dynamics, McDonnell Douglas, and North American. Four other firms - Boeing, Lockheed, Grumman, and Northrop - had participated in the concept formulation effort but did not submit proposals. In November-December the Aeronautical Systems Division and the F-15 program office (established in August 1966) began evaluating the four proposals and negotiating with the firms. On December 30, 1968, Dr Flax announced the award of $15.4 million in contracts for contract definition to all bidders except General Dynamics. They were asked to submit technical proposals - including the projected cost of the aircraft and a development schedule - by the end of June 1969.

As contract definition began, a question arose over the number of competitors the US Air Force should maintain and for what length of time. In February 1969, shortly after becoming Secretary of the US Air Force, Dr Robert Seamans issued new guidelines to reduce the number of contractors. These guidelines required the firms to indicate the number of workers and the amounts of other resources that each proposed to devote to the competition and updated information on their planning and organization, their record of correcting deficiencies, and the effect their other aircraft programs might exert on the F-15. Dr Seamans also assigned Robert Charles, his assistant for Installations and Logistics (I&L) to investigate each firm's ability to assume the commitments and risks required by the new contractual approach. Secretary Seamans hoped the information obtained would enable him to eliminate one of the three contractors by April and another by September 1969.

Dr Foster, on the other hand, believed that the three F-15 contestants should continue to compete for a longer period, and he suggested the US Air Force extend the competition to January 1970. He thought the delay would be well worth the extra costs; that the extended competition might prove a good investment in terms of the final cost of the F-15 development contract.

The F-15 contract negotiations, conducted during November and December 1969, involved a total of six contracts with three airframe companies. Each company also signed contracts with two engine manufacturers. The idea was to have all these contracts in force, pending first the US Air Force's selection of an airframe builder and, following that, the engine developer. In effect, the US Air Force obtained commitments without having to wait for the results of the competitions.

THE F-15 PROGRAM OFFICE

Several years before contract negotiations began, the US Air Force established an F-X special projects office at Wright Patterson US Air Force Base, Ohio, to oversee development of both the F-X and A-X close air support aircraft. The office first came under ASD's Deputy for Advanced Systems Planning, more specifically, the General Purpose Planning Division. Established on August 12, 1966, it was initially headed by Colonel Robert Daly and allotted 17 'validated' positions.

Throughout 1967, Colonel Daly's staff was preoccupied with the task of preparing the F-X concept formulation documents. These ranged from a description of the program to documents dealing with planning, programming, and funding. The System Program Office (SPO) also provided extensive data to satisfy OSD's demands for a proposed joint US Air Force and Navy advanced tactical fighter. Headquarters USAF established January 1969 as the target date to begin contract definition, and in May 1968 the A-X (later A-10) close support fighter SPO was separated from the F-X and set-up as a separate entity. In June 1968 Colonel Robert White became the new SPO director.

An important change that affected the F-15 SPO took place on July 11, 1969, when Brigadier General designee Benjamin Bellis was named its new director, replacing Colonel White who became his deputy. General Bellis was one of the US Air Force's most experienced R&D managers.

SOURCE SELECTION

On July 1, 1969, the three F-15 airframe competitors - Fairchild-Hiller, McDonnell-Douglas, and North American - submitted technical proposals and two months later, on August 30, their cost proposals. The Source Selection Evaluation Board (SSEB) headed by General Bellis, then evaluated these bids, examining 87 separate factors under four major categories - technology, logistics, operations, and management. They rated the competitors in each category and, without making a recommendation, submitted the raw data to a Source Selection Advisory Council (SSAC), comprised of representatives from the user commands and chaired by Major General Lee Gossick, the ASD commander. The council then applied a set of previously established weighting factors that they had defined in June 1969, before the start of the evaluation. Although rating the contractors in the four major categories, the council, did not select a winner. Instead, it forwarded the scores through the Air Staff to Secretary of the US Air Force, Dr Robert Seamans, who as Source Selection Authority (SSA), was the final decision-maker.

PROJECT FOCUS

During this evaluation, however, Secretary Packard directed the US Air Force to minimize costs by making a thorough final review (Project Focus) of the F-15 program requirements. He acknowledged that the review, in taking several months to complete, would delay the F-15 IOC date, but he felt this compromise would be worthwhile if it avoided costly mistakes. The Deputy Secretary also clamped a $1 billion per year spending limit on the F-15 program and directed that Project Focus be completed by mid-November 1969 to avoid disturbing the source-selection process. Sensitive to criticism of the F-15 program, he especially examined these items: recommendations for alternate avionics; simpler data and reporting systems; reducing

Fourth prototype F-15A 71-0284 was used for weapons testing and was the first aircraft fitted with the 20mm M61 cannon. Note the high-speed camera fitted to the aft underside of the fuselage. US Air Force

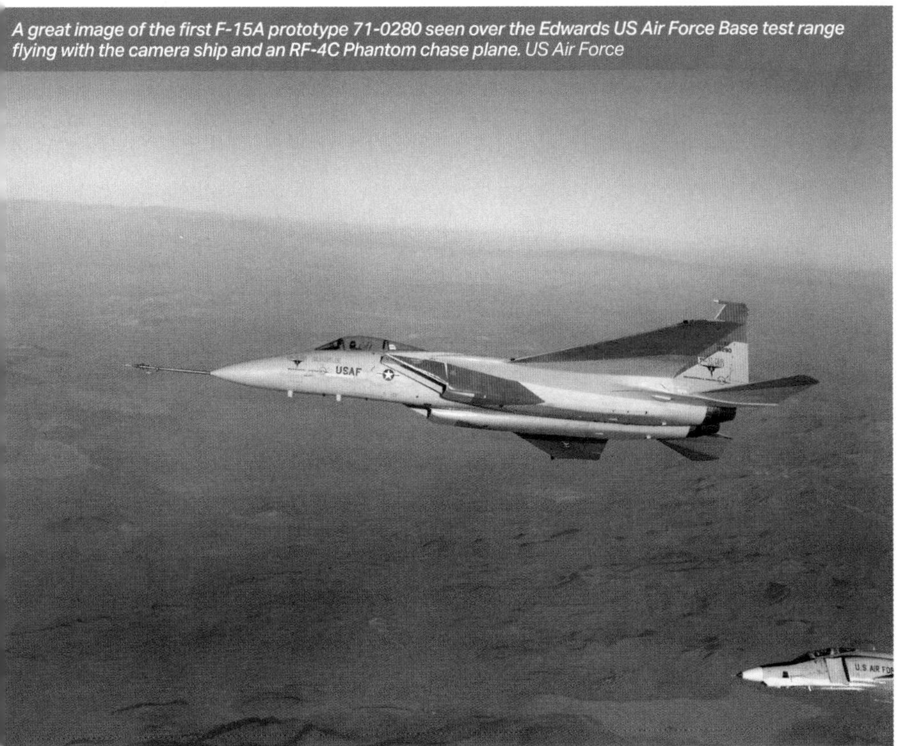

A great image of the first F-15A prototype 71-0280 seen over the Edwards US Air Force Base test range flying with the camera ship and an RF-4C Phantom chase plane. US Air Force

airframe costs; alternate subsystems; and contractor suggestions.

Meanwhile, the US Air Force had acted promptly to meet Secretary Packard's call for a program review. General Bellis established a Program Evaluation Group (PEG) to define a $1 billion annual production plan, restrict development funds in FY1970 through 1972, and cut unit production costs. The group quickly suggested a long list of items to reduce F-15 costs by more than $1.5 million per aircraft. As a result of Project Focus the following actions were taken to hold down F-15 costs.

AIRCRAFT

Windshield bird-proof requirement deleted
Use 'Fail Safe' in lieu of 'Fail Operational' flight control system
Use F-105 escape seat technology
Install M61 gun (provide for 25mm gun)
Delete nuclear curtain
Delete pressure suit
Delete voice warning
Eliminate soft field landing requirement
Evaluate material usage
Reduce training requirements
Reduce MIS satellite complex
Reduce data requirements

AVIONICS

Replace vertical tapes with round dials

IN THE RADAR

Deleted parametric amplifiers
Deleted low PRF long range mode
Reduce threshold of sizable clutter
Simplified digital signal processor
Reduced air-to-ground map range
Deleted inflight fault isolation
Eliminated hydraulic boresight
Reduced computation requirement, eliminated one computer Using off-the-shelf communications equipment
Reduced inertial navigation accuracy requirements Using off-the-shelf navigational instrument
Reduced IFF and TEWS packages

TEST

Combined testing where common instrumentation existed
Reduced flight test hours
Reduced spares and spare parts
Modified system demonstrations
Deleted high performance test bed
Reduced air-to-ground delivery qualifications

The US Air Force asked its contractors to update their costs proposals in October 1969. McDonnell Douglas, reducing its cost estimate by about $500,000, submitted the lowest revised bid. The cost review continued throughout the F-15 project and a subsequent General Accounting Office (GAO) report in July 1970 credited it with about $1 billion savings. In December 1969, encouraged by the work of Project Focus, Secretary Packard authorized the US Air Force to go forward with the F-15 development.

MCDONNELL WINS

Secretary Seamans, having announced the award of the F-15 contract to McDonnell-Douglas on December 23, 1969, estimated that the development phase, including the design and fabrication of 20 aircraft, would cost $1.1 billion. Donald Malvern, McDonnell's F-15 general manager, reported that the firm had already spent five million man-hours in winning the F-15 contract. His team of between 200 and 1,000 people had worked for two years examining over 100 alternative designs with thousands of variations. From an economic standpoint, the F-15 contract 'saved' one third of the company's 33,000 jobs in the St Louis, Missouri, area even though in 1968 McDonnell led the nation's aerospace firms, earning $95 million on revenues of $3. 6 billion. The F-15 contract also promised to increase McDonnell's sagging commercial airliner sales and absorb the slack of lowered F-4 production.

As for the losers, North American planned to lay off 1,500 of its 6,500 Los Angeles Division employees. Ironically, the company had reduced its Advanced Manned Strategic Aircraft (AMSA) effort in May 1969 to concentrate on the F-15 competition but went on to win the bomber project in June 1970. The smallest of the three companies, Fairchild-Hiller, failed to establish itself as a major defence contractor, though it did win the A-X (A-10) competition in 1973.

SUB-SYSTEMS

Although USAF officials had rejected a prototype competition for the F-15 airframe contract, they readily pursued this approach for the aircraft's subsystems. The explanation was simple since the engine, radar, and short-range missile were the critical subsystems,

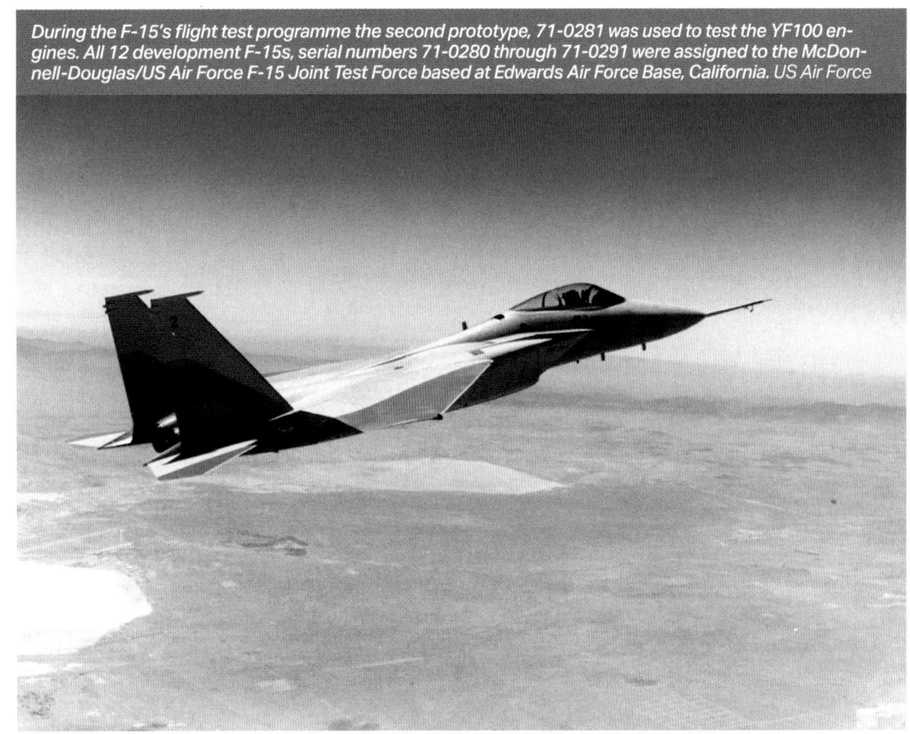

During the F-15's flight test programme the second prototype, 71-0281 was used to test the YF100 engines. All 12 development F-15s, serial numbers 71-0280 through 71-0291 were assigned to the McDonnell-Douglas/US Air Force F-15 Joint Test Force based at Edwards Air Force Base, California. US Air Force

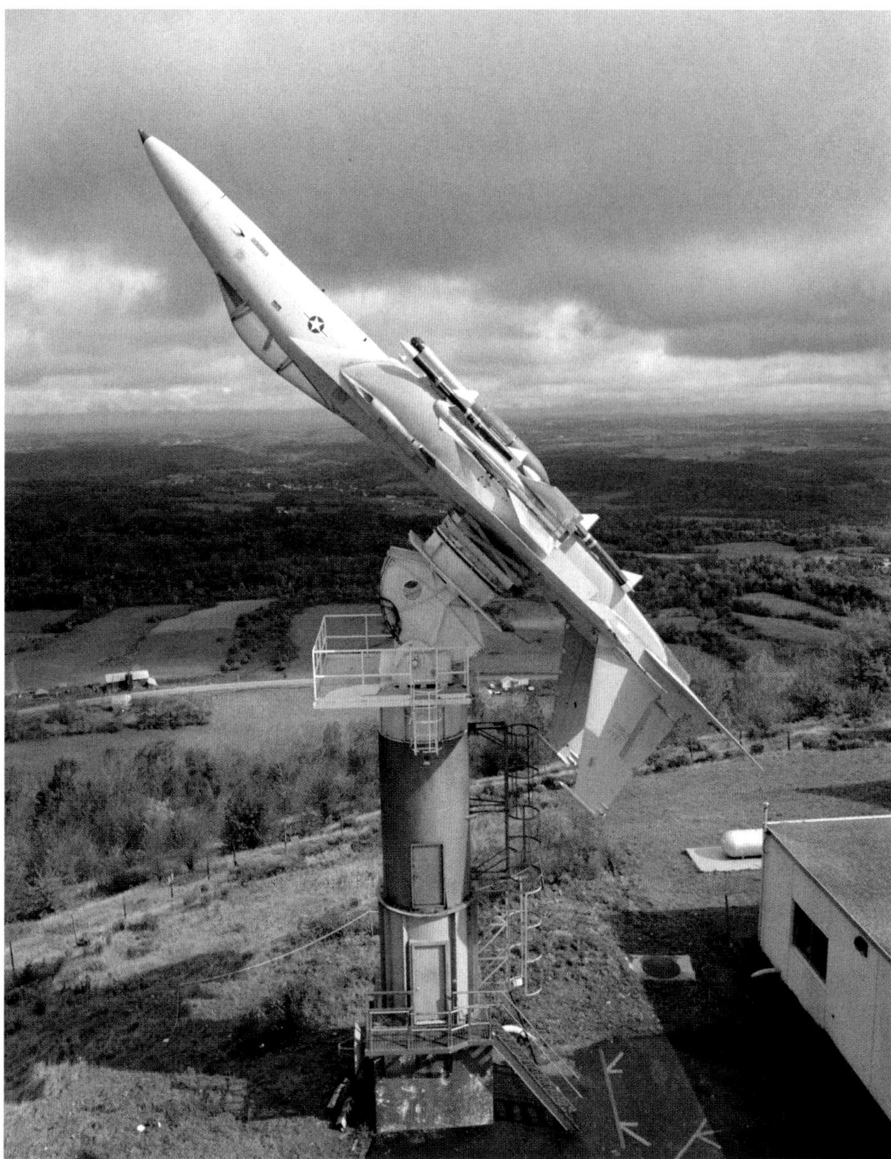

Dr Foster also sought to retain for OSD final source selection authority, but the services were able to persuade him to delegate this authority to them.

On April 8, 1968, requests for proposal were sent to General Electric, Pratt & Whitney, and the Allison Division of General Motors. Revised in July, these requests outlined a 'barebones' $125 million program to develop a prototype competition among several contractors would reduce program costs and risks. System contractors were to be selected based on proof-testing and demonstration of subsystem prototypes.

LEFT AND BELOW: *Early production-standard F-15A Eagle 73-0112 mounted upside down on a pedestal at the Rome Air Development Center's Newport test site - part of Griffiss Air Force Base, New York. The two photographs were taken during evaluation of a radar warning system pod mounted on the fuselage in comparison with the aircraft's onboard radar warning system. US Air Force*

THE ENGINE

In December 1967, the US Air Force and Navy agreed to conduct a joint engine-development program. Their goal was to develop a high-performance afterburning turbofan Advanced Technology Engine (ATE), drawing upon the experience gained in the development of the lift-cruise engine of the US-West German V/STOL and AMSA bomber programs. The proposed new engine was required to produce 40 percent more thrust and weigh 25 percent less than the 12-year-old TF30 engine used in the F-111. New lightweight materials and improved design promised more efficient compressor stage-loading and higher turbine temperatures. Generally, military specifications called for the new engine to develop more than 20,000 pounds thrust and have a 9 to 1 thrust-to-weight ratio.

It featured a 22 to 1 pressure ratio in only 10 stages, whereas, by comparison, the J79 (F-4 aircraft engine) had an overall 14 to 1 ratio involving 17 compressor stages.

From the start of the engine project, the US Air Force and Navy disagreed about its management. In early 1968 the US Air Force proposed establishing within one service a joint engine-program office (JEPO) run according to its management procedures and subject only to change for operational and logistical requirements of the other service. This proposal, reflecting the US Air Force's single-management concept for the F-15 program, had precedent in other joint projects such as the Navy's purchase of US Air Force J79 engines for its F-4s. On the other hand, the Navy favoured single-source procurement and creation of a Joint Executive Committee to oversee separate project offices in each service. The US Air Force rejected this proposal, fearing that it would produce divergent engine configurations without yielding the desired cost savings.

The situation reached an impasse, with neither side willing to budge from its position. At one point in this stalemate, US Air Force and Navy officials convened a meeting where they simply read their respective position statements and then left without discussing their differences. The issue was partially resolved in April 1968, when Dr Foster named the US Air Force executive agent to manage the Initial Engine Development Program (IEDP), but he left open his decision on management of the final development phase.

22,300-pound thrust engine weighing 2,790 pounds and having a 'common core' gas generator interchangeable with the Navy's F-14 engine. At the end of August, OSD authorized the award of two 18-month contracts totalling $117.45 million to General Electric and Pratt & Whitney. The US Air Force contract was a composite cost-plus and fixed-type arrangement like that for the F-15 airframe, except for a different set of fees and ceiling prices. The Navy's contract, on the other hand, specified fixed prices for both the development and production phases.

Jointly funded by the US Air Force and Navy, the contracts authorized each company to build two prototype engines - one for each service. The purpose was not merely to develop different engines, but to fulfil each service's thrust requirements. Since the Navy's proposed aircraft was heavier than the F-15, it required a larger engine. Although both the US Air Force and Navy engine models were to be designed, only one of the models would be built. However, since the Navy planned to use the TF30 engine in its F-14 prototype, the services agreed that only the US Air Force engine model and some components of the

Navy model would be built initially. Later, though, both General Electric and Pratt & Whitney invested their own funds to build the Navy's engine model as well.

In November 1968, the plan for a joint engine program appeared to flounder when the US Air Force and Navy announced they would conduct separate contracting and funding arrangements at the end of the initial engine development phase. Dr Foster, however, wished to retain one service as the project manager, at least until both services' engine models met their Military Qualification Test (MQT). Accepting his ruling, the US Air Force and Navy agreed to proceed as before but postponed submitting an engine development plan for the remaining phases of the program. Although they appreciated and endorsed the advantages of a joint effort, the US Air Force and Navy preferred to await further definition of the F-X and VFX airframe designs before making a commitment.

SOURCE SELECTION

Meanwhile, the US Air Force and Navy agreed to share source selection authority for the engine. General Goldsworthy, the ASD commander (and his successor, Major General Lee Gossick), represented the US Air Force, with Admiral J. T Walker, Naval Air Systems Commander, being his Navy counterpart. Both parties agreed that in the event of conflict between engine and airframe selections, authority would revert to the service secretaries. A similar arrangement governed the source selection board and council, with US Air Force and Navy personnel serving as co-chairmen for the two groups.

Even with initial engine source selection under way, the services continued to ignore program management during the final phase. Dr Foster did not forget and in August 1969 he warned the R&D secretaries that unless they submitted an acceptable management plan by the engine qualification test date, OSD would reassume source selection authority.

Despite this deadline, the two services continued to disagree. The US Air Force argued that changing the JEPO arrangement would disturb the F-15 program whereas the Navy insisted on having 'plant cognizance' [having management authority] if Pratt & Whitney won the engine contract. With each side claiming its approach was the more economical and efficient one, the issue festered until October 1969, when both asked Secretary Packard for a ruling. Some two months later he advised the service secretaries that the US Air Force would continue as lead service for the engine development, threatening to take back selection authority if they were unable to choose a winner. General Ferguson and Admiral I. J. Gallantin, Chief of Naval Materiel Command, finally resolved the issue by negotiating an US Air ForceNavy agreement to continue the JEPO under the F-15 office and to have General Bellis respond to the Naval Materiel Command chief on F-14 matters and to AFSC on the F-15.

Earlier, in June and July 1969, the two engine contractors submitted technical and cost proposals. The Source Selection Evaluation Board began its study of them on July 7 but did not complete the task until January 30, 1970, because the contractors were late submitting their design substantiation data. In February 1970, after reviewing this data. the board designated the Pratt & Whitney design as 'clearly superior to the General Electric System.' After the Source Selection authority (Secretary Seamans) also chose Pratt & Whitney, that company received the formal award on March 1, 1970, authorizing the US Air Force and Navy to sign separate engine contracts with it.

The US Air Force engine model, designated the F100-PW-100, was an augmented twin-spool, axial-flow gas turbine that delivered more than 22,000 pounds thrust and weighed less than 2,800 pounds. The Navy version of the ATE - the F401-PW-400 - used the same 'common core' as the F100, including common compressors, a smokeless annular combustor, and two high-pressure stages. The two engines differed in the fan, afterburner, and compressor sections. The addition in the Navy model of a stub compressor in front of the main compresso increased engine airflow but, by raising its weight, lowered the engine thrustto-weight ratio. The F401 generated over 27,000 pounds of thrust and weighed under 3,500 pounds.

F-15A 71-0287 was used for spin recovery and angle of attack trials and fuel system testing. US Air Force

Five F-15A Eagles assigned to the 405th Tactical Training Wing based at Luke Air Force Base, Arizona. Luke was the first location to host operational F-15 Eagles. US Air Force

In January 1969, the Navy changed the size of its engine because the F-14B (formerly VFX-2) would be larger than planned. Although the change increased the difference between the F-15 and F-14 engines, the common core approach remained intact and did not affect costs. The Navy's change required increased airflow to raise thrust from 25,000 to 27,100 pounds for the GE version and from 26,000 to 28,160 pounds for the P&W design. GE's solution was to raise the fan bypass ratio, whereas P&W added a stub stage to the fan to supercharge the common core.

Developing the Advanced Technology Engine was the main problem in an otherwise exemplary F-15 program. In November 1970, because of F-14 funding cuts, the Navy pared its engine request from 179 to 69 units in FY1972 through 1974. Since the larger number of engines set the original cost, this cut required a new formula with a higher price per engine for the US Air Force. In the spring of 1971, the Navy further cut its order to 58 engines to fit the lagging F-14B airframe schedule. Then, on June 22, a new Navy decision to buy 301 F-14A's (the model that used the TF30 engine) cancelled the remaining 58 engines and voided the joint Navy-US Air Force engine production contract.

Earlier, in February 1971, Pratt & Whitney projected a $65 million cost overrun in the engine funding for FY1973.

Although the JEPO stood fast then, advising the contractor that no more funds were available, these new circumstances forced the US Air Force to rewrite its own engine production contract. The new agreement raised US Air Force costs by about $532 million. Under this revised program, development milestones for the F401 engine slipped from February to December for the Preliminary Flight Rating Test, from February to June 1973 for the military qualification test and from June 1972 to mid-1974 for the delivery of production models.

The Advanced Technology Engine also suffered from several technical problems. At the start of the development program, there were two compressor designs: the primary aerodynamic compressor Series I engine, and the advanced aerodynamic compressor Series II. In October 1970 both services favoured Series I because it was lighter and on schedule. However, by mid-1971, when it appeared that the Series I version would not meet its full production requirements, the services revived Series II. The US Air Force eventually installed Series I in its first five test aircraft and Series II in all remaining test aircraft and in its F-15 production models.

In February 1972, the YF100 (Series I) engine passed its PFRT milestone on schedule, in time for the F-15's first flight in July. The US Air Force rated Series I superior in thrust-to-weight, fuel consumption pressure ratio per stage, and turbine temperature levels. Meanwhile, in August 1972, the US Air Force suspended MQT testing three times for the Series II engine - an early warning of the many engine troubles to come in 1973.

RADAR AND ARMAMENT

The F-15's remaining subsystems were open to competitive development. After soliciting industry bids on August 8, 1968, the US Air Force selected Westinghouse Electric and Hughes Aircraft in November to develop, produce, and test models of the attack radar subsystem.

McDonnell-Douglas, the airframe contractor, was responsible for selecting the winner of the 20-month competition after flight testing and evaluating both radar prototypes. The US Air Force wanted a lightweight, highly reliable advanced design suitable for one-man operation. The radar's capabilities were to include long-range detection and tracking of small, high-speed objects approaching from upper altitudes down to 'tree-top' level. The radar was to send tracking data to a central on-board computer for accurate launching of the aircraft's missiles. For close in dogfights, the radar was to acquire targets automatically on the head-up display so that the pilot would not have to do this task manually. In July and August 1970, McDonnell-Douglas conducted more than 100 flights to test competing radar units aboard its modified RB-66 aircraft. With US Air Force approval, McDonnell awarded Hughes Aircraft the radar contract in September.

To cut costs. the US Air Force ordered another thorough 'scrub down' of the F-15 requirements. Starting in July 1970. a panel headed by Major General Jewell Maxwell reviewed the avionics and armaments. focusing on three items: (1) the Tactical Electronic Warning System (TEWS), whose development cost the panel favoured separating from the F-15 program; (2) Target Identification Sensor-Electronic Optical (TISEO), a device for target identification beyond visual range; and (3) the AIM-7-E2-missile, a backup for the AIM-7F Sparrow. The US Air Force adopted the panel's recommendation to eliminate the last two systems.

The F-15's armament included both missiles and an internal cannon. The US Air Force added the gun on the advice of veteran pilots and Vietnam returnees as well considering the Israeli success [a 54-0 air-to-air victory over Arab fighters] with cannon in the June 1967 'Six-Day War'.

Though the primary gun for the F-15 was the M61 Vulcan (a 20mm Gatlingtype cannon used in Vietnam), the US Air Force also began a longterm project to develop a 25mm cannon using caseless ammunition. In the spring of 1968, it selected Philco-Ford and General Electric to design a prototype of the advanced gun designated the GAU-7A Improved Aerial Gun System [with greater velocity and projectile weight]. The $36 million fixed-price competition ended in November 1971, when Philco-Ford won the contract.

The US Air Force also proposed to equip the F-15 with a new short-range missile (SRM) for use against manoeuvring fighters at close range. In March 1970, the US Air Force selected three contractors - Philco-Ford, Hughes Aircraft, and General Dynamics - to begin competitive prototype development. Six months later, however, the US Air Force cancelled the SRM because of rising costs, agreeing with the Navy to substitute an improved version of the Sidewinder missile.

DISSENT AND DECISION

Despite USAF attempts to stem criticism of the F-15, basic differences arose within and outside the Pentagon over the kind of aircraft to acquire. The US Air Force was especially sensitive to criticism because of competition with the Navy to get funds for an air superiority fighter. Having established the F-15's basic requirements, the US Air Force decided to 'speak with one voice' and not tolerate any dissent. Nevertheless, criticism of the F-15 made the US Air Force re-examine the project and design an aircraft markedly superior to the one it had promoted at the beginning of the program.

F-15 VS FOXBAT AND THE F-14

In urging development of the F-15, the US Air Force was pressed to explain the aircraft's alleged 'inferiority' to the Soviet *Foxbat*. Industry sources claimed the F-15 could not defeat the high-speed, high-altitude *Foxbat* (Mach 3+ at 80,000 ft) and urged scrapping the F-15 program. General Rhodarmer's team however, convinced Congress that, in terms of manoeuvrability, the F-15 was superior to any existing or projected Soviet aircraft. They noted its superior manoeuvrability in air combat, emphasizing the F-15's decided edge in such key dogfight factors as wing loading and thrust-to-weight ratio.

Criticism of the F-15 prodded the US Air Force to look at other aircraft. It established a joint flight-test program with the National Aeronautics and Space Administration (NASA) to experiment with the YF-12 - a high-speed, high-altitude fighter developed by Kelly Johnson of Lockheed. The US Air Force also funded Mr Johnson to study an advanced tactical fighter combining the speed advantages of the YF-12 and the F-15's superior manoeuvrability. Eventually, the US Air Force concluded that the cost of developing such an aircraft would be prohibitive and that the F-15's manoeuvrability, radar, and 'shoot-up' Sparrow missiles could defeat the *Foxbat*. Describing the *Foxbat* as a technological threat only, the US Air Force remained convinced of the F-15 's ability to 'out-fly, out-fight, and out-fox the rest.'

In authorizing development of the next generation tactical fighters, OSD generally presented the F-15 and F-14 as non-competitive aircraft. It saw the F-14 providing the Navy with a long-range missile capability (AWG-9 Phoenix) for fleet air defence and the F-14 variants performing 'other fighter roles,' whereas the

F-15A 74-0111/LA at Luke Air Force Base in November 1974 assigned to the 555th Tactical Fighter Training Squadron. US Air Force

-15 was to achieve overall air superiority. When ongressmen asked the inevitable question s to which of the two aircraft would win in a ogfight, neither the Navy nor the US Air Force vas hesitant to advance its own candidate.

However, in the spring of 1969, General IcConnell and Admiral Thomas Moore, hief of Naval Operations, agreed to toe the SD line - namely, that the two aircraft were ntended for different missions. Whenever the ssue did arise, the US Air Force highlighted ne F-15 's manoeuvrability advantage and the nission differences between it and the F-14.

ODIFICATIONS AND FIRST FLIGHT

riticism of the F-15's design assumptions, nough viewed as a threat by some military fficials, actually produced distinct dvantages. These challenges obliged the US ir Force to re-examine the aircraft's design nore critically and 'scrub out' extraneous equirements. In particular, NASA's role as consultant during the source selection nd its independent laboratory evaluation ncovered certain deficiencies that might therwise have gone unnoticed. For example, ASA found the F-15's subsonic drag level vas higher than reported. To correct this roblem, designers removed the ventral fins nd enlarged the vertical fin. General Bellis, estifying in the spring of 1971 before the enate Armed Services Committee, discussed he major design changes in the F-15 since its contract award: "The radome has been made more symmetrical to enhance the radar performance. Cowl fences have been added to the upper outer edge of the inlet to improve directional stability. The inlets have been refined. The bluntness of the cowl lip has been changed.. .The wing and horizontal tail were both moved five inches... to improve aircraft balance and maintain the desired handling qualities and stability....To improve the external aerodynamics, the aft section of the aircraft has undergone some refinement; this includes modified lines, ventral removal, and increased vertical tail height."

On June 26, 1972, the F-15 made its ceremonial debut at McDonnell-Douglas' St Louis plant. Appropriately painted in 'air superiority blue' and christened the Eagle, it was hailed as America's first air superiority fighter since the F-86 appeared some 20 years earlier.

The F-15's next milestone event - the first flight - occurred on July 27 when Irving Burrows of McDonnell-Douglas piloted the fighter on a 50-minute maiden flight over Edwards US Air Force Base, California. All systems 'worked as expected,' and the Eagle attained 12,000 feet and about 320 miles per hour. This event also launched the F-15's flight-test program, which continued on schedule without any significant problems through its 1,000th flight in November 1973. By that date, the F-15 had flown above 60,000 feet at speeds over Mach 2.3.

The flight-test program, perhaps the most rigorous one ever conducted in American aviation, included wind-tunnel, structural-materials, and flight-simulation tests. Category I testing by the contractor involved 12 aircraft instrumented for specific flights. For example, the No.1 prototype tested the aircraft's stability and control characteristics, aerodynamic parameters, and provided a 'quick look' at the YF100 pre-production engines and overall aircraft performance.

Prototypes 13 through 20 were designated for US Air Force use in Category II testing. The US Air Force and McDonnell-Douglas also shared test time on five of the first 12 prototypes. Flight testing took place at three locations - Edwards US Air Force Base, Eglin US Air Force Base, Florida, and the McDonnell-Douglas airfield in St. Louis, Missouri. The test team at Edwards included seven TAC pilots and six ASD pilots. Wind tunnel tests occurred at Arnold Engineering Development Center near Tullahoma, Tennessee.

NASA supported the F-15 flight-test program by evaluating three-eighths scale models of remotely piloted research vehicles (RPRVs). The aluminium and fibreglass RPRV's, 23.8 feet long with 16-foot wingspans and weighing 2,000 pounds, were dropped from 45,000 feet at 175 knots from B-52 aircraft. These trials provided invaluable data that enhanced the safety of the full-scale tests later.

Claws, Vampires

During his US Air Force career, Daniel Leaf commanded a flight, two squadrons, an operations group, two fighter wings, and directed joint operations. He is also an experienced F-15 pilot.

F-15A Eagles in formation over Arizona during a photo mission. Each aircraft is painted with tail markings for commanders of the 405th Tactical Training Wing and each assigned squadron (near to far) the 461st, 426th, 405th (wing), 550th, and 555th Tactical Fighter Training Squadrons. US Air Force

and Nickels

Daniel 'Fig' Leaf completed pilot training with the 14th Flying Training Wing at Columbus Air Force Base, Mississippi in November 1975. He subsequently completed training on the F-4 Phantom with the 35th Tactical Fighter Wing based at George Air Force Base, California before serving with the 49th Tactical Fighter Wing based at Holloman Air Force Base, New Mexico. Following two years flying the OV-10 Bronco forward air control aircraft, and a one-year tour working for Headquarters Pacific Air Forces at Hickam Air Force Base, Hawaii, in the spring of 1981, Dan started flying the F-15 Eagle with the 405th Tactical Training Wing at Luke Air Force Base, Arizona.

After completing the nine-week course at Luke, Fig was assigned to the 18th Tactical Fighter Wing based at Kadena Air Base, Okinawa for his first operational tour. He was in the second group of F-15 pilots assigned to Kadena, joined the 44th Tactical Fighter Squadron 'Vampires', and served as an F-15C pilot, instructor pilot, and flight commander, and later as the wing's standardisation and evaluation branch chief during a four-year tour.

Fig then attended the US Army Command and General Staff College at Fort Leavenworth, Kansas before returning to the F-15 at Luke serving as an instructor pilot and operations officer with the 426th Tactical Fighter Training Squadron 'Killer Claws'. He then commanded the 555th Tactical Fighter Training Squadron 'Triple Nickel', and later the 58th Operations Support Squadron, all components of the 58th Tactical Training Wing, completing the four-year tour in May 1992. Fig was then sent to the Air War College at Maxwell Air Force Base,

F-15A Eagles assigned to the 405th Tactical Training Wing in formation over Arizona during a photo mission. US Air Force

Alabama before moving to Langley Air Force Base, Virginia to serve as the 1st Operations Group deputy commander and subsequently as its commander on a two-year assignment which ended in July 1995. His next assignment was with the Joint Task Force Southwest Asia, at Riyadh, Saudi Arabia, with the J-3 operations directorate. This was the last job in which he flew the F-15 Eagle, an aircraft assigned to the Eglin-based 33rd Tactical Fighter Wing on deployment to the US Central Command's area of operation in support of Operation Southern Watch. Fig's flying career continued as an F-16C pilot when he served as the commander of both the 20th Fighter Wing, based at Shaw Air Force Base, South Carolina through November 1998 and the 31st Fighter Wing based at Aviano Air Base, Italy through January 2000. Fig subsequently served in command roles with combatant and major command.

Recalling his first impression of the F-15 aircraft, Fig said: "The F-15 was an elegant aeroplane to fly, not easy to maximise your mastery of the aircraft but just to fly, and it was so much better than any other fighter at the time, such that when we conducted dissimilar training against other types of aeroplanes it was usually an easy fight. During my time, that set the stage for how F-15 pilots viewed the aeroplane in its operational application."

VAMPIRES

Fig's first operational F-15 assignment was with the 44th Tactical Fighter Squadron based at Kadena in the South China Sea. According to Fig, Kadena's location a long way from Headquarters Pacific Air Forces and even further from Headquarters, Tactical Air Command, allowed the squadron and the wing to innovate.

He qualified as mission capable in the F-15 after a programme of qualification training with the squadron and soon became a flight lead, then an instructor pilot and flight commander. Discussing squadron operations, Fig said: "We deployed a lot during that time. Regular deployments were to Clark Air Base in the Philippines for Exercise Cope Thunder and to Osan Air Base in the Republic of Korea to sit the PARPRO alert [see below] to protect the Peacetime

> "In 1982 we started flying big formations, from two or four-ships to 12-ships to packages comprising as many as 48 F-15s."

Airborne Reconnaissance Programme aircraft, primarily SR-71s and U-2s, and to Gwangju Air Base in South Korea for exercises like Team Spirit, a joint exercise between the US and the Republic of Korea."

PARPRO flights were flown on the periphery of North Korea and other nations. They were legal and could be undertaken on the authority of the theatre commander. The first PARPRO flights took place on the periphery of the USSR in 1946.

Discussing employment of the F-15 at the time, Fig said: "The 18th Tactical Fighter Wing at Kadena was leading the evolution of air superiority tactics in the US Air Force. There had been a European-influenced mindset that involved a lot of low altitude employment to avoid radars and surface-to-air missiles. Such tactics had risks because you were flying down in the anti-aircraft artillery and small arms engagement zones. So, in 1982 we started flying big formations, from two or four-ships to 12-ships to packages comprising as many as 48 F-15s. We also moved the employment to medium altitude. It was deemed to be more survivable against surface threats and would maximise the F-15's killing power against the air threat.

"That was the shift the F-15 brought to US tactical air forces. In fact, eight pilots were qualified to drop Mk84 and Mk82 general purpose bombs off wing pylons. The aircraft had the necessary wiring and software in the weapons computer and the head-up display for aiming. We called it sports bombing, because it wasn't central to our air superiority mission, but the notion was from our prescient 313th Air Division Commander based at Kadena, then Brigadier General Tom McInerney, later lieutenant general. The notion was that the enemy would quickly stop flying, and we'd have to go find them to kill them. That was a pretty bold notion in 1982-1983 but it's exactly what happened in Operation Desert Storm; Iraqi Air Force pilots didn't take off, because they realised that they'd get their ass kicked.

Lieutenant General Daniel 'Fig' Leaf. US Air Force

"We even flew missions with communications out, so we would fly a four-ship, and except for emergency and contingency situations, we did not talk on the radio but employed an effective four-ship mission, which was unheard of until that time. And we proved we could do that, and felt quite certain of the capabilities, not just as pilots, but those enabled by the incredible F-15. The reality of the F-15 is 104 to zero, the aeroplane remains undefeated in aerial combat. That statistic influenced how we viewed the aeroplane, and how the adversaries viewed the F-15, and I'll provide an operational example.

"It's exactly what happened in Operation Desert Storm; Iraqi Air Force pilots didn't take off, because they realised that they'd get their ass kicked."

Note the configuration of the tail numbers. Each aircraft has the last four digits of the serial number displayed rather than the usual three digits; the fourth digit being the second digit of the fiscal year. US Air Force.

On August 31, 1983, I was in Seoul in the Republic of Korea, showing my new boss, at the time Brigadier General Mike Nelson, around the country while continuing his checkout programme in the F-15.

"Early in the morning of September 1, 1983, the Soviet Air Force found it necessary in their minds to shoot down a Korean Airlines Boeing 747, flight KL007, with over 200 people, including a US congressman, on board, who were tragically all killed. Because we were visiting a US Air Force unit early that morning, General Nelson and I quickly learnt about what had happened, probably in more detail than most. Promptly we returned to Kadena. When I checked in with my squadron's operation desk as we taxied in, I was told to get to the squadron right away and to not bother debriefing. I knew that we were going to be doing something and that it must be related to the shootdown of KL007. As it turned out, the 44th Tactical Fighter Squadron was tasked to deploy five F-15Cs to Misawa Air Base, Japan to provide any protection necessary for the search effort of KL007 and prevent Soviet interference.

"I arrived at Misawa onboard a C-141 around midnight. One of the F-15s had to divert to Yokota Air Base because the aircraft hit a fruit bat which damaged an engine, ironic given the 44th Tactical Fighter Squadron's Vampires nickname. So, we had four F-15s fully loaded with live missiles parked near the end of the runway with some maintainers and not much else. At the time there was no US Air Force fighter wing based at Misawa, the F-16-equipped 432nd Tactical Fighter Wing was activated there in July 1984.

"It was notable that the F-15 aircraft deployed to Misawa were not assigned to the 44th but the 12th Tactical Fighter Squadron. Its aircraft had recently been through an upgrade and had greater radar capability. They had better jets, but we had better pilots! We had Colonel Gary Baber, the wing's deputy commander for operations, and our squadron commander, Colonel Joe Lee Burns, four flight commanders and some folks from my flight, and we didn't have much guidance. My wingman, then Captain Mike Oakes, and I sat down on the ramp underneath a light to plan. There were three reference points progressively positioned ever closer to Soviet airspace: spear, pistol, and rifle which we used as references. We determined our employment doctrine, including what the radar responsibilities were, and what kind of shots we would take if we had to launch missiles, all largely hypothetical at that point.

"At 0200 on September 2, we were ready to go on alert status and briefed our plan to Colonel Baber. Providing guidance, he said, 'as soon as you get airborne, request clearance to the first point, spear, if they clear you out of spear immediately ask for clearance further north to the second point, pistol. If you get cleared beyond pistol, jettison your wing tanks. If you get to the third point, rifle, request clearance to engage. If you get clearance, jettison your centreline tank, arm hot and kill MiGs'. That's all the guidance we had. Mike and I thought we were in on the start of World War Three. Despite the potential for facing a lot of Soviet fighter aircraft we had no fear, the aeroplane and its weapons gave us that confidence. There was no place we'd rather have been than to take on the Far East Soviet Air Force and kick their ass after they shot down a civilian airliner.

> **"There was no place we'd rather have been than to take on the Far East Soviet Air Force and kick their ass after they shot down a civilian airliner."**

"Mike and I had sat on alert for six hours and then handed off the alert to Colonel Joe Lee Burns, the squadron commander and Captain Keith Reisner, a fellow flight commander, without scrambling. Sometime into their alert period, Colonel Burns and Captain Reisner were ordered to scramble and head north. As they taxied, Captain Reisner had a big survival knife between his teeth which typified the attitude pilots had to flying the F-15. We were told by our intelligence officers, true or not, that the Soviet Air Force knew that F-15s were launching from Misawa, so they aborted the two MiG-23s on take-off from Dolinsk-Sokol Air Base. That was perhaps the imposing air dominance that enabled the F-15 to achieve 104 aerial kills for no losses. There's no other aeroplane that's dominated its environment in its time like the F-15."

EAGLE EXPERIENCES

On August 15, 1988, Fig had flown a training sortie in his role as an instructor pilot. While taxiing back to parking the master caution light illuminated, advising the pilot to check hydraulics. Explaining, Fig said: "I looked at the panel which showed a utility A failure, so I pulled the emergency brake and steer handle, depressed the paddle switch, and kept it depressed so I could pull over to get the aeroplane chocked and shut down. I happened to be near the transient aircraft ramp, so I asked ground control to contact the people working at the transient alert office to bring me some chocks, because the F-15 has no parking brake, which is a rare negative thing about the F-15.

"I saw an airman dragging chocks out, but he was in no hurry. As he walked under

Three F-15C Eagles assigned to the 44th Expeditionary Fighter Squadron based at Kadena Air Base, Japan, during a temporary deployment to Korat Royal Thai Air Force Base, Thailand during Exercise Cope Tiger 2011. US Air Force

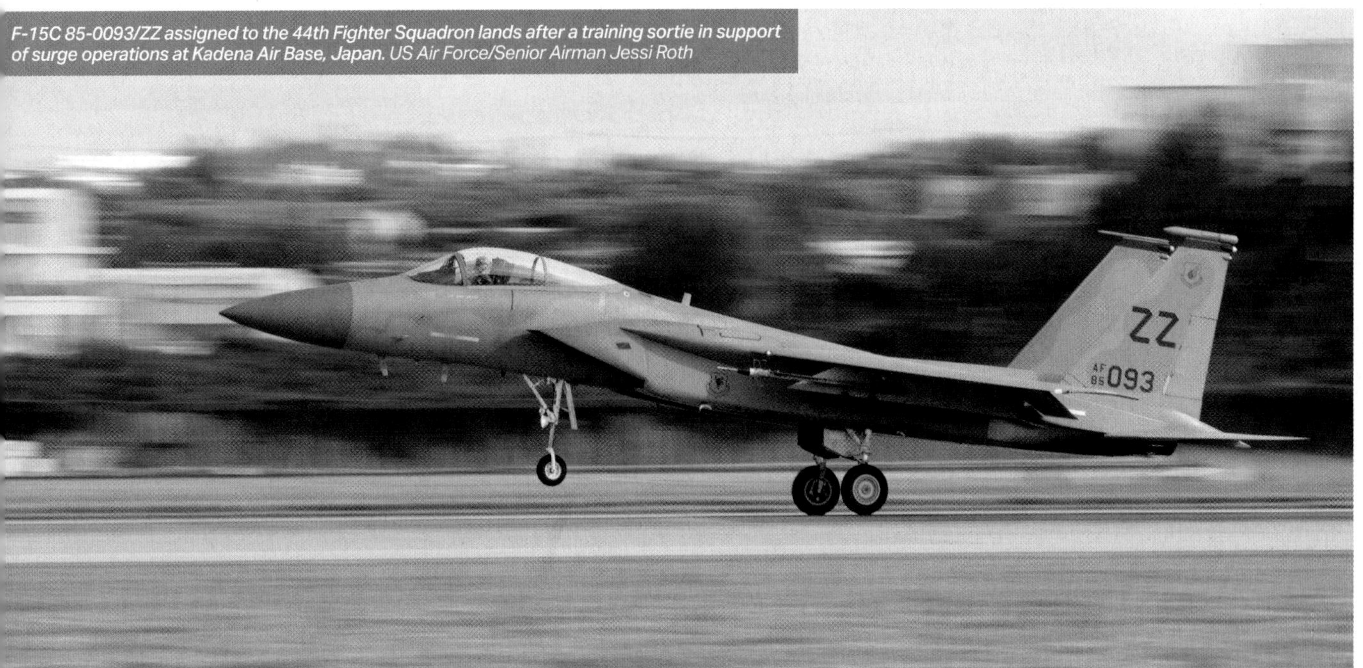
F-15C 85-0093/ZZ assigned to the 44th Fighter Squadron lands after a training sortie in support of surge operations at Kadena Air Base, Japan. US Air Force/Senior Airman Jessi Roth

he tip of the left wing, the master caution ight illuminated, advising me to check ıydraulics for a utility B failure, a potential otal utility failure. Suddenly the emergency ›rake pedals lost their pressure, so I had no ›rake and opposite me was an F-4 Phantom ›arked on the transient ramp. My aircraft started to roll, so perhaps I should have shut down both engines and accepted the ender bender with the F-4 but that didn't come naturally to me. In addition to having ıo brake, I had no nose gear steering so I ncreased the power on the left engine in the ıope the aircraft would move to the left. My ıircraft lurched away from the F-4 without ı collision but started rolling faster with the ncreased power.

"In my mind, the cognitive dissonance of thinking 'this shouldn't be happening' was annoying. I tried moving every switch I could think of that might be relevant and decided it was too complex to get back to a runway and take a cable. Instead, I decided to taxi the aircraft to an area of the ramp with an intersection, where one taxiway had an uphill slope. I shut down the left engine to reduce the forward thrust, continued rolling forward to the intersection where my plan was to bear left. At the point I was about to do that a blue security forces pickup truck with two airmen inside crossed my path. Clearly, neither of them thought I would bear left, so I was faced with a choice. Stick with my plan to turn and inevitably hit the truck and kill all three of us, or collide

"As they taxied, Captain Reisner had a big survival knife between his teeth which typified the attitude pilots had to flying the F-15."

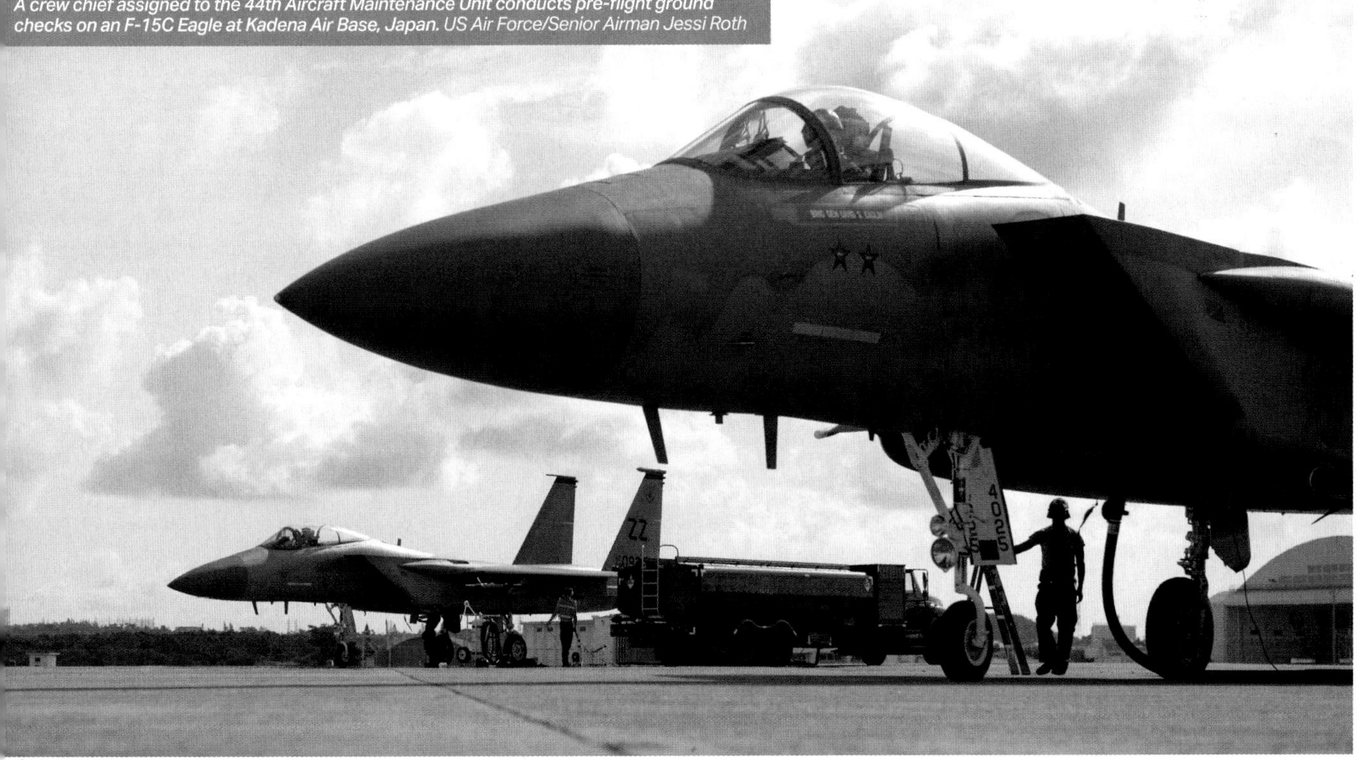
A crew chief assigned to the 44th Aircraft Maintenance Unit conducts pre-flight ground checks on an F-15C Eagle at Kadena Air Base, Japan. US Air Force/Senior Airman Jessi Roth

> **"Suddenly the emergency brake pedals lost their pressure, so I had no brake and opposite me was an F-4 Phantom parked on the transient ramp."**

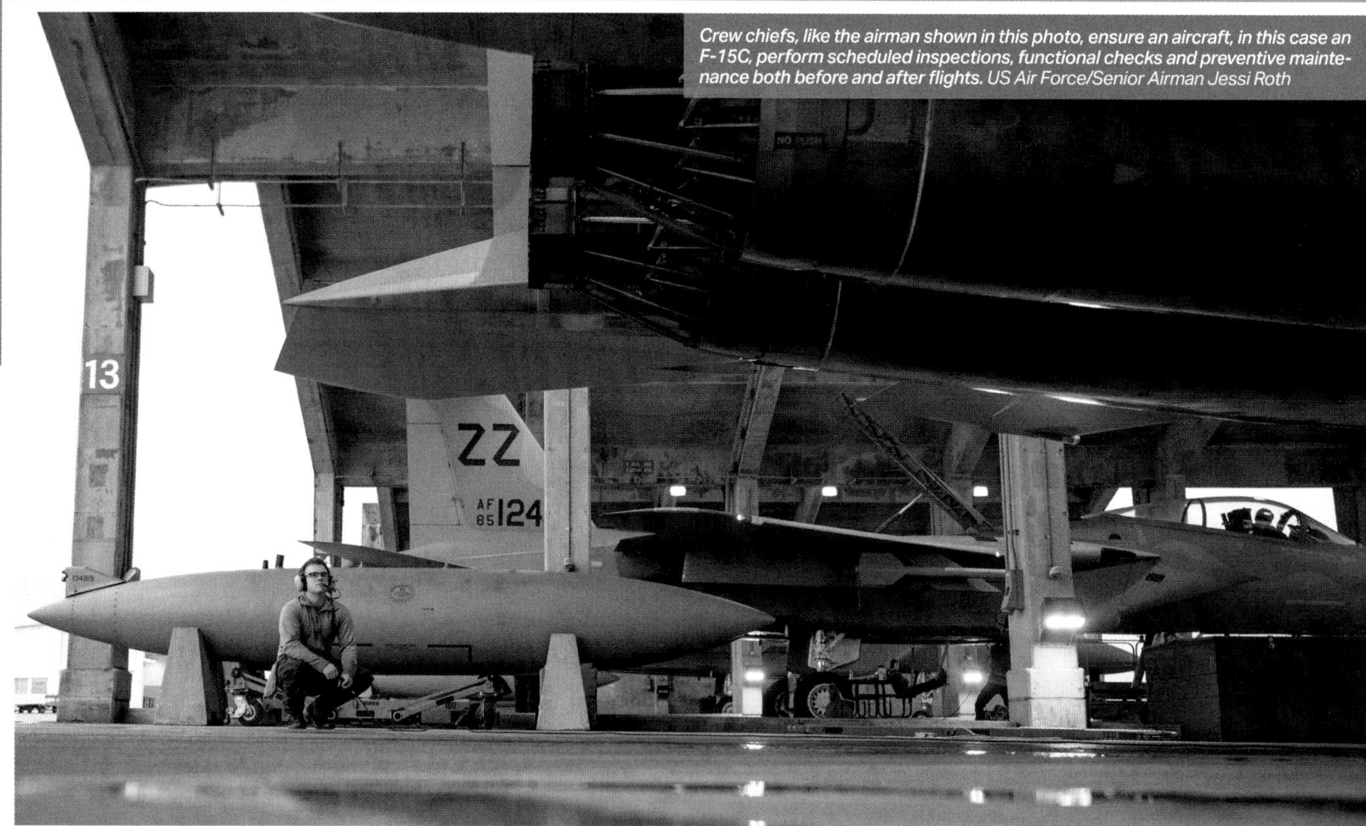

Crew chiefs, like the airman shown in this photo, ensure an aircraft, in this case an F-15C, perform scheduled inspections, functional checks and preventive maintenance both before and after flights. US Air Force/Senior Airman Jessi Roth

with an F-16 assigned to the 314th Tactical Fighter Training Squadron parked right ahead of me and kill me and destroy two aircraft?

"At the very last moment, the pick-up truck began to fade from my view, which meant I might not hit it. So, I pushed the right throttle into the afterburner range and closed my eyes because I didn't want to see the explosion that was bound to kill. Under the additional power, my aeroplane lurched to the left, there was no explosion because I'd cleared the F-16 and yanked the power to idle. There were five light poles ahead of me, with an unpaved and uncultivated area beyond, so I applied a burst of power, then shut down the right engine, rolled the 42-feet wide aircraft between two of the poles and onto the uncultivated ground. The nose gear sunk into the soft dirt, pivoted around the strut, and the aircraft shuddered to a stop, and more to the point, I was alive! I got out of the aeroplane and knelt on the ground, shaking like a tuning fork, then sat down so I wouldn't fall over.

"It transpired that the issue was a previously undocumented failure mode on the left main landing gear. My aeroplane had a three-quarter inch wide gash on the tail plane, and the only damage to the F-16 was a broken wing tip light on its corresponding right wing, very superficial damage for what could have happened. This made no sense because the tail plane and the wing of my aircraft should have impacted the F-16 as per my envisioned catastrophe. I accepted I was very lucky.

An F-15C Eagle assigned to the 44th Fighter Squadron seen on take-off from Kadena Air Base. Japan. US Air Force/SSgt Peter Reft

F-15 MULTI-STAGE IMPROVEMENT PROGRAM

According to Joe Baugher's excellent US Air Force website: "Under the Multi-Stage Improvement Program, upgrades were progressively incorporated onto the production line and retrofitted to aircraft already in service. MSIP II was integrated on F-15C and F-15D aircraft, the main elements were the APG-70 radar and the AIM-120 AMRAAM air-to-air missile.

The APG-70 has increased radar data processor memory, increased processing speed, each support Non-Cooperative Target Recognition (NCTR) technology, multiple bandwidths for high-resolution ground mapping using SAR technology and new radar modes, such as track-while-scan, a low probability of intercept capability, which makes it possible for it to detect and direct attacks on enemy aircraft without its emissions being easily seen by the enemy.

MSIP II also included

- *The Seek Talk program, which was designed to reduce the vulnerability of the F-15's UHF radios to enemy jamming by introducing spread spectrum techniques and the use of a null steering antenna.*
- *The Joint Tactical Information Distribution System (JTIDS) to provide high-capacity, reliable, and jam-proof information distribution between various aircraft and command and control centres.*
- *Global Positioning Satellite (GPS).*
- *A new multi-function display armament control panel was introduced.*
- *New stick-top and throttle grips.*
- *The ALQ-128 Electronic Warfare Warning Set (EWWS) was modified into the more capable Tactical Electronic Warfare System (TEWS) with an ALQ-135 electronic countermeasures set and an upgraded ALR-56C radar warning receiver.*
- *An overload warning system was provided to prevent pilots from accidentally exceeding 9g during combat manoeuvring.*

"Fast forward ten years when serving as the new commander of the 31st Fighter Wing at Aviano and I was talking with Lieutenant Colonel David Goldfein one of the squadron commanders. He asked me if I was at Luke when that guy had that hydraulic failure and how he had used differential throttles to try and avoid a collision? 'That was me,' I said. He then said he saw the incident. Turns out he was in an F-16 in the row behind the damaged aircraft waiting to taxi on his first solo flight in the F-16. He told me that when I applied the power on the right engine, there was so much thrust, it lifted the right main gear off the tarmac and lifted the right side of my aeroplane which moved over the F-16 avoiding a serious collision. In short, that's why I'm alive."

When Fig served as the director of operations for Joint Task Force Southwest Asia in Riyadh, Saudi Arabia, he had the opportunity to fly an F-15C on a mission to enforce the no-fly zone over southern Iraq, checking for Iraqi aircraft as part of Operation Southern Watch. Explaining the mission, Fig said: "It was a very slow day. There was nothing happening. Then on the last excursion near the limits of our patrol, a master caution light illuminated indicating a series of hydraulic failures that were nonsensical with the hydraulic built-in test and not mirrored by the hydraulic pressure gauges. But at least one of the systems was fluctuating and eventually showed

Patrolling the South China Sea, three F-15C Eagles assigned to the Vampires. US Air Force

> **"The F-15 remains an amazing aeroplane and operationally relevant because it was designed with room for growth."**

ero on the gauge. I turned south and headed or Al Jaber Air Base in Kuwait. Upon arrival I owered the arrestor hook and took a cable: the edundancy of the aeroplane saved me."

-15 SENTIMENTS

iscussing the F-15 aircraft, its mission, and its apability in that mission, Fig said: "The aircraft ad so much capability, and as a community ve were so focused on the air superiority nission and being the best at it. We had high tandards, because the aeroplane demanded igh standards. During my time at Luke serving s an instructor pilot and squadron commander, ve had a 9% attrition rate of students who'd one well enough in pilot training to get an -15 assignment but couldn't meet standards n the B-course and washed out for a variety f reasons, such as defensive basic fighter nanoeuvres, which is hard, or getting into the hree-dimensional air-to-air environment.

"The aeroplane demanded the best. When was assigned to Langley Air Force Base as the 1st Operations Group deputy commander and later group commander, I had to transition from the early version of the F-15, which was extraordinarily capable to fly, to the version upgraded in the Multi-Stage Improvement Programme dubbed MSIP (see panel), which had an improved radar. MSIP was such a quantum leap in killing power, and for me proved to be the most difficult transition I ever did in the air force, in terms of squeezing the most out of the aircraft and weapon system.

"When I took my instructor pilot mission commander upgrade on the MSIP II aircraft, I already had over 1,000 hours in the F-15, but my check ride with one of the squadron commanders sucked. I said he should not pass me based on that check ride, because I was not good enough with the upgraded aeroplane to be a mission commander. Attaining that upgrade required more training sorties, and my performance in the aircraft improved."

Concluding, Fig said: "The F-15 remains an amazing aeroplane and operationally relevant because it was designed with room for growth. But that growth is only partially attributable to the evolution of technology because no growth could have happened if the F-15 wasn't such a fundamentally sound platform."

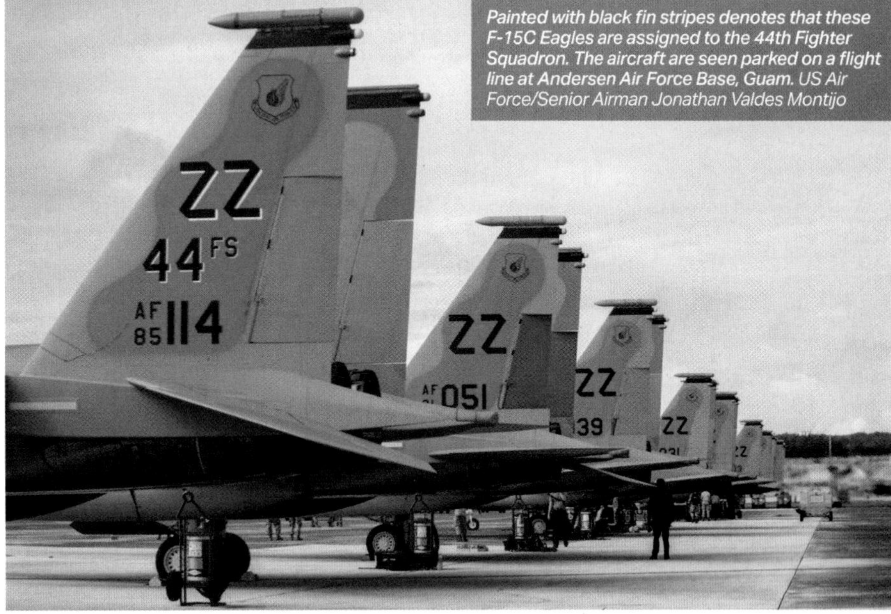

Painted with black fin stripes denotes that these F-15C Eagles are assigned to the 44th Fighter Squadron. The aircraft are seen parked on a flight line at Andersen Air Force Base, Guam. US Air Force/Senior Airman Jonathan Valdes Montijo

F-15C 78-0522/ZZ assigned to the then 44th Tactical Fighter Squadron taxies past a row of B-1B bombers assigned to the 28th Bomb Wing at Andersen Air Force Base, Guam during Exercise Giant Warrior 1989. US Air Force/TSgt Lee Schading

MiG Killer

Flying was not a childhood dream for Cesar Rodriguez, which is ironic given his career as a pilot in the USAF saw him amass nearly 3,400 hours and achieved three MiG kills to his name.

While flying wasn't a childhood dream for Cesar Rodriguez, he did well enough at college to flight school. He took the plunge and never looked back.

Cesar completed air force pilot training with the 71st Flying Training Wing based at Vance Air Force Base in Oklahoma in 1983. Discussing his course, Cesar said: "When reviewing my records from the T-37, my instructor pilot said that if I wanted to fly fighter aircraft, I had to do 100 times better than what I had done in the T-37. He said he would help me but not hold my hand because the fighter community would not do that. He got me thinking and I refocused my effort to do well enough to be selected for fighters. At the end of the 12-month course I finished in the middle of my class.

"I was selected for the A-10, completed the B-course with the 355th Tactical Training Wing based at Davis-Monthan Air Force Base, Arizona and was then assigned to Suwon Air Base in the Republic of Korea to serve with the 25th Tactical Fighter Squadron. My tour was scheduled to be a one-year remote tour, but I completed my upgrades and stayed for a second year when I completed upgrades to four-ship flight lead, mission commander, and instructor pilot."

Cesar was then assigned to Holloman Air Force Base, New Mexico as an instructor pilot on the lead-in fighter training course with the 479th Tactical Training Wing. On completion of his Holloman tour, Cesar had to compete for another aeroplane, and he opted for the F-15. He was selected and assigned to the 325th Tactical Fighter Wing based at Tyndall Air Force

"Operating F-15C MSIP aircraft opened a lot of doors to places and flying experiences that were for me, as a young F-15 pilot, complex and demanding."

F-15A 75-0045/EG assigned to the 58th Tactical Fighter Squadron on a training mission over the Gulf of Mexico. US Air Force

ase, Florida. He completed the TX-course ith the 2nd Tactical Fighter Training Squadron merican Beagles' flying the F-15A-model. His ubsequent first operational F-15 assignment as with the 33rd Tactical Fighter Wing based t Eglin Air Force Base, Florida where he served ith 58th Tactical Fighter Squadron 'Gorillas' tarting in the autumn of 1988.

Cesar recalled his early impression of the t, saying: "With its power, and stick and udder control, you felt the aeroplane did hat you asked of it. As you learnt more about e aeroplane, you could ask more of the eroplane, and yet remain within the limits of your body. It was a relatively easy aeroplane to fly, the complexity of the F-15 was in how you employed it. F-15 pilots like Paco Geisler, Rob 'Cheese' Graeter, and Jon 'JB' Kelk were masterful in how they employed the aeroplane.

"As a mid-level captain, flying an aeroplane equipped with a radar for the first time, I had to do a lot of learning about how to fly and monitor my radar and employ the radar to its advantages, and ultimately to simulate employing weapons. Fortunately, we had simulators that provided a full 180 degrees of vision which enabled a lot of the radar formation flying, so your hands, eyes and feet were synchronized in fighting with the aeroplane.

"At Eglin, the 33rd Tactical Fighter Wing operated the new F-15C MSIP [Multi-Stage Improvement Program], which presented another steep learning curve, because the difference between an A-model and a C-model was truly night and day. The new MSIP aeroplane had a different wing, a different fly-by-wire flight control system, and different engines. MSIP aircraft were more maintenance friendly than A-model aircraft thanks to built-in test [BIT] failure readers that isolated which black box needed to be replaced.

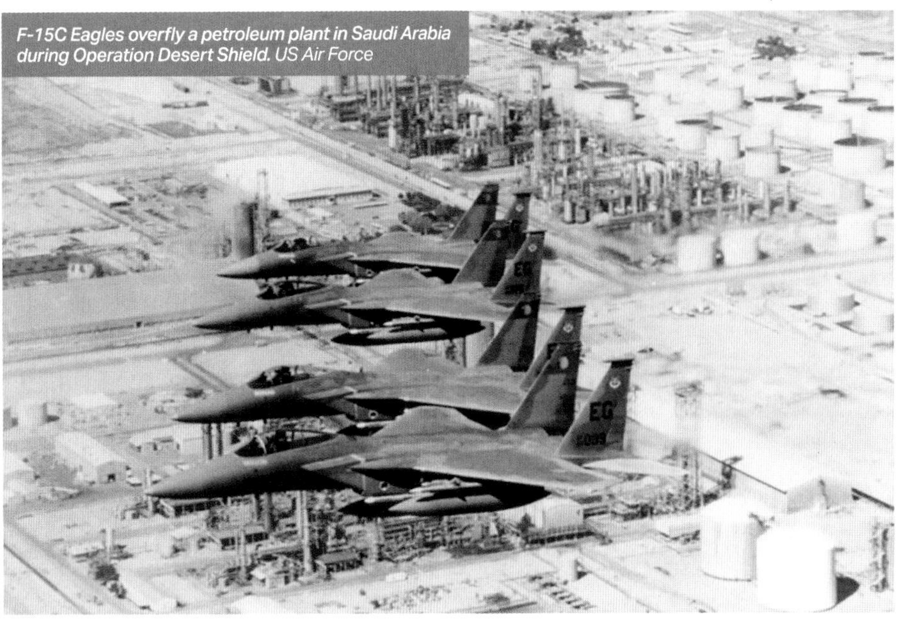
F-15C Eagles overfly a petroleum plant in Saudi Arabia during Operation Desert Shield. US Air Force

"Because the 58th Tactical Fighter Squadron had the newest F-15s in the air force, we undertook a lot of training and testing, because nobody else had the assets that we had. So, we completed a lot of trips to Nellis Air Force Base in support of both the Fighter Weapons School and the 422nd Test and Evaluation Squadron. Operating F-15C MSIP aircraft opened a lot of doors to places and flying experiences that were for me, as a young F-15 pilot, complex and demanding. Consequently, in December 1989, our squadron was selected to set up a CAP on the west side of Cuba to protect the armada of airlifters flying to Panama during Operation Just Cause, the code name for the US invasion of Panama. And of course, in 1990 when Saddam Hussein's forces invaded Kuwait, the squadron was given its marching orders to deploy to Saudi Arabia.

"On the afternoon when the order came for us to prepare to deploy our maintenance teams hit it out of the park in the sense of getting the aeroplanes ready. Our MSIP aircraft were fitted with guarded red switches, the wires for which had to be cut, and testing was required to make sure they were ready to go. All weapons loaded on the jets were BIT-checked and made ready to go. For the first 48 hours, the work completed by our maintenance team to prepare the aeroplanes was rock solid. Looking at the squadron scheduling board, as each aircraft entered its inspection cycle, a couple of hours later, it was marked green.

"At the time we deployed, a huge hurricane had developed in the middle of the Atlantic which forced us to route to Charleston, South Carolina and then head directly across the Atlantic toward Morocco and the Straits of Gibraltar supported by a bridge of tankers.

"We flew for 20-plus hours direct from Eglin to Tabuk Air Base in Saudi Arabia. When the first of our pilots shut down at Tabuk he tried to stand up, but it was clear he needed some help after sitting in the seat on a quarter inch of foam for 20 plus hours, which was not

"When the first of our pilots shut down at Tabuk he tried to stand up, but it was clear he needed some help after sitting in the seat on a quarter inch of foam for 20 plus hours."

Two F-15C Eagles assigned to the 493rd Fighter Squadron taxi to parking at RAF Lakenheath, England. US Air Force

An F-15C Eagle seen during an engine run in the hush house at Eglin Air Force Base, Florida. US Air Force

easy. So, our maintenance airmen placed A stands next to the cockpit, once we'd popped the lid open, the crew chiefs grabbed you by the shoulders to help you stand up and do a couple of squats back and forth to get your muscles pumping blood again before they helped you get out of the aeroplane. After a quick check by our flight surgeon to make sure you could touch your toes and flex your back, we slowly walked to the maintenance debrief and turned in the jet's paperwork.

"Within 24 hours of landing, we had the first four jets with crews on alert ready to respond, and within 72 hours we were flying DCA CAPs. We were in the earliest stages of a defensive air campaign in the early stages of Desert Shield flying different HVA CAPs to monitor activities inside Iraq. Once the southern borders of Kuwait were secure, we held a 24/7 presence. Desert Shield was an evolving operation and there was no Desert Storm on the books per se, so we didn't know what timeframes we were dealing with. So, we got permission from the CAOC to unload weapons from eight jets which we used for training missions, for example dissimilar air combat with Royal Saudi Air Force F-5s. Just before Christmas, we started to get wind of a bigger plan, our weapons officer kept us briefed on the plan as it was evolving, and then the role of the F-15 in a night one scenario, and how it might play out.

"Once the first weeks' worth of missions was authored in an ATO format, our mission commanders had conversations back and forth between the different bases on their roles, responsibilities, expectations, go, no go, criteria. Given we had MSIP standard F-15s, we took the air-to-air mission commander role for most of the missions. In some cases, the default mission commander was assigned to the F-15 unit that was closest to the operating area based at either Al Kharj, Dharan and Tabuk.

"I was flying as part of the last four-ship of F-15s to get airborne from Tabuk under Desert Shield when Operation Desert Storm started. We were tasked to do a series of manoeuvres at the border to see how the Iraqis responded, and it was clear that they were not anticipating anything. At the end of our mission, we went to a different tanker track, because by that time, aircraft assigned to Desert Storm were getting airborne, and going to tankers in the track usually used, so we had to save enough gas to make it home. I got four hours of sleep and returned to the squadron to fly Desert Storm missions.

"They were different to any of the Desert Shield missions. We were crossing into

"Within 24 hours of landing, we had the first four jets with crews on alert ready to respond, and within 72 hours we were flying DCA CAPs."

Two F-15C Eagles assigned to the 493rd Fighter Squadron taxi to parking at Nellis Air Force Base, Nevada during Exercise Red Flag. US Air Force

US Air Force

aq, one of the first calls you made was naster arm hot' because you were flying ith an entourage of live air-to-air missiles. very night-one mission is an emotionally hallenging event that each pilot must deal ith individually. Of course, you're nervous, ut the F-15 community had always built quadron standards to the highest possible, o that the night-one mission should feel like n average day of flying, except somebody's ying to kill you, and you're going to try nd kill somebody. The flight lead-wingman elationship also takes on a different ura because you don't want to lose your ingman. And, of course, the last thing you ant to do is have a blue-on-blue missile ngagement.

"Some things were easy to debrief in a aining scenario, but now they were for real. ll kinds of thoughts screamed through your ead, and when the canopy came down your eart rate was up with adrenaline pumping round your body, so it was a completely ifferent experience for the body."

IRST MIG SHOOTDOWN

n January 19, 1991, Cesar, and his wingman oth scored air-to-air victories against an Iraqi iG-29. They were originally on a defensive ounter air mission in western Iraq. They had een there for nearly five hours when the ommand-and-control mission commander n board the AWACS contacted them with a -tasking to provide DCA for a strike package r a new target. Part of a four-ship, two F-15s ere to join the strike package and two were hold a CAP.

Discussing the sequence of events, Cesar said: "I sent three and four to the tanker and then on the CAP followed by one and two to the tanker who then joined the strike package. Another four-ship of F-15s was out front in the pre-strike role and we were the post-strike sweep. The four-ship of F-15s up front encountered a series of MiG-29s and Mirage F1s and ended up scoring three air-to-air kills. In that engagement, they jettisoned their fuel tanks and didn't have enough gas to make it all the way to the designated target area.

"The strike mission commander decided to continue with the mission and asked us to fly out front as the pre-strike sweep. Once out in front the radar picture showed enemy fighters to the west and northwest of the target, and more to the northeast of the target.

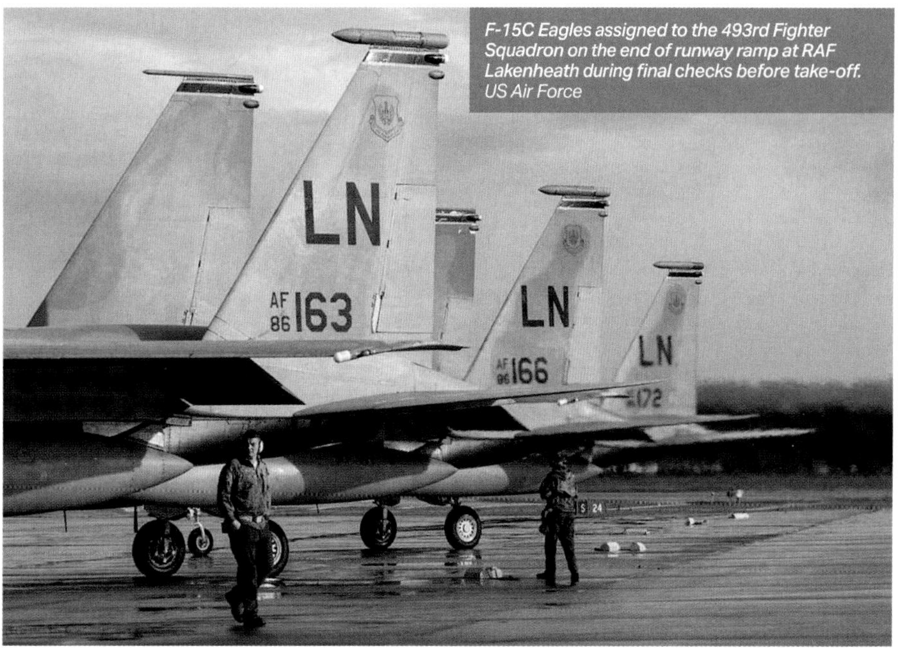

F-15C Eagles assigned to the 493rd Fighter Squadron on the end of runway ramp at RAF Lakenheath during final checks before take-off. US Air Force

Two F-15C Eagles fly in close formation behind a KC-135 tanker over the vast desert of Saudi Arabia during Operation Desert Shield. US Air Force

The eastern group were the closest to the target area. We weren't sure if the western group were committed to our spot, so I asked the AWACS controller to monitor them.

"We headed to the eastern group. We couldn't break out their close formation until a 15-mile range. They executed a perfect beam manoeuvre followed by a drag manoeuvre. When they went into the beam, our radars had a problem keeping up with it. Once they started dragging back toward their home base, we picked them up again. Unbeknownst to us, they had set us up for a SAM trap.

"We were 12 miles directly behind them at 35,000 feet. If we'd have taken an AIM-7 shot, we could have shot them, but of course an AIM-7 requires you to hold the missile all the way till impact. That would have pulled us into Baghdad. At that time, the AWACS controller called to notify us of some pop-up contacts off my left wing. I couldn't see them on my radar, it was locked into the formation. My attention was grabbed when the formation was just eight miles away which made us very nervous, so when I broke lock, I hit the jettison button for my tanks and rolled my aeroplane to 330, I got an auto gun lock on the first target, which was exactly eight miles off my wing. I started to go through the ID matrix with four or five steps left before I could take a shot. At about six miles the MiG locked me up, so I started to defend, and did a split S from 35,000 feet. My goal was to get below the MiG's altitude and release a bunch of chaff to try to decoy my aeroplane. Then I handed off the information to my wingman who found the same MiG and started to go through the ID matrix, then he got another confirmation from a Rivet Joint on our frequency.

"Descending from 35,000 feet, I got down to just below 1,000 feet, my wingman completed the ID matrix, called Fox 1, and took an AIM-7 Sparrow shot against the MiG. I saw the missile come off his aeroplane, cut across my tails and around to my high five o'clock position, at which point the missile stopped smoking. As I levelled off, I followed the smoke trail to about my right three o'clock. That was the first time I saw the MiG at a range of three miles. I rolled out trying to do a defensive beam manoeuvre on his aeroplane, then my wingman's missile hit the MiG-29 and it exploded right in front of me.

"I called 'splash one' for my wingman's air-to-air kill. Then the AWACS controller called us again to notify us of a second group of MiGs. I directed the formation north. I'm at low altitude, my wingman's at 25,000 feet. We both locked onto the second group and started the ID matrix, I showed hostile in my jet, my wingman showed friendly in his jet. We redid a second ID matrix we got the same results, neither of us carried a spike, so I conducted a visual intercept on the MiG, started a low-to-high conversion, put the MiG in my target detection box inside the HUD field of view, looked to see if I could tell anything about the target, it looked like a western fighter.

"I committed to the intercept and ended up passing about 500 feet off the MiG's left wing. That's when I confirmed it was a brown and green camouflage MiG-29 with an Iraqi flag on the tail. In a classic two circle fight, I pulled towards his tail, my team was jamming his GCI frequency, a couple seconds later, he started a left turn, by which time I climbed into the vertical, went over on my back, started my turn to the inside of his circle, and then started to drive a position to set me up behind his three-nine line [the invisible line that runs from one wing to the other].

"My biggest challenge was to control my speed and secure my three-nine position. After about a turn and a half, I was perched behind his three-nine line, and on the outside of his turn, both in a left-hand turn, descending. As I passed through 1,000 feet above the desert floor, I pulled to the inside to put a radar lock on him. He was at about 600 feet, decided to roll inverted, started a Split S without his afterburners lit, he tried to get his nose above the horizon but hit the desert floor. The strike package headed south, there are no other MiGs in the area, so we headed south back to Tabuk."

> **"One of the first calls you made was 'master arm hot' because you were flying with an entourage of live air-to-air missiles."**

SECOND MIG SHOOTDOWN

Seven days after his first air-to-air victory against an Iraqi MiG, Cesar was involved in another encounter with one, as he explained: "When we took off from Tabuk on January 26, 1991, we hit the clouds at about 600 feet, and we didn't break out till we were above 30,000 feet. Storms dominated the entire AOR. The only aeroplanes that flew that day were F-15s providing defensive counter air protection to the HVA which were monitoring every ground, electronic, and airborne movement the Iraqis were making. While on a CAP just to the west of Baghdad, an AWACS controller confirmed there was some air activity in the area near airfields H1 and H2 located in western Iraq.

The pilot of 493rd Fighter Squadron F-15C 86-0164/LN takes off from RAF Lakenheath in full afterburner. US Air Force

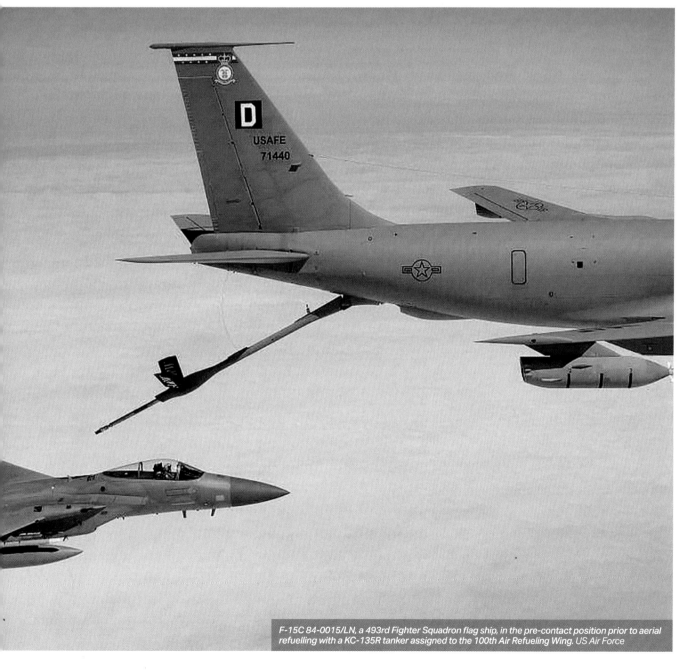

F-15C 84-0015/LN, a 493rd Fighter Squadron flag ship, in the pre-contact position prior to aerial refuelling with a KC-135R tanker assigned to the 100th Air Refueling Wing. US Air Force

The pilot of F-15C Eagle 79-0075/EG assigned to the 58th Fighter Squadron, prepares to fire an AIM-120 Advanced Medium Range Air-to-Air missile at a QF-4 full-scale aerial target drone during a weapons evaluation mission over the Gulf of Mexico. US Air Force/MSgt Michael Ammons

"The flight lead was the late Rory Drager [Hoser], his wingman Tony Schiavi [Chemo], I was number three and my wingman for the day was Bruce Till [Roto]. We headed west-southwest at high altitude, thinking we were going to be shooting through the clouds if there were any Iraqi aircraft airborne.

"At 40 miles, we saw some movement on the airfield. One aeroplane, a MiG-23, got airborne. We also found a big gap in the weather, so we descended, broke out at 20,000 feet, and continued down to 15,000 feet. There were now three Iraqi MiG-23s in a VIC formation [like a V] with one aircraft in the lead and one more aircraft spaced by about 1,000ft off the left and right wing of the lead jet. Rory called out the radar picture, we assigned our individual responsibilities based on that radar picture. Rory had the number one target, Chemo the northernmost and I had the southernmost. Roto was targeting to check there were no other aircraft in that formation.

"At about 12 miles, we could see the MiG-23s, Rory took the first shot, followed shortly thereafter by Chemo and then me. The AIM-7 missiles came off the aeroplanes and descended toward the desert floor: the MiGs were as low as 100 feet above the ground. The first missile went underneath the lead MiG, its pilot started a gentle left hand turn to the north, we were surprised it didn't blow up. As the lead MIG turned to the north, the two wingmen both turned to the east and the southeast. The northbound MiG's engines started generating a smoke trail, so Rory peeled off to the north and uncaged [activated the seeker to freely rotate to track the target] an AIM-9 Sidewinder against the MiG, and while getting ready to hit the pickle button, the MIG blew up. The missiles launched by me and Chemo both hit the nose of each aeroplane, both exploded into fireballs and totally obliterated each MiG-23. We quickly turned to the south, headed towards a tanker, and then retuned back to the CAP until four more F-15s arrived to take up the CAP. We gave the pilots a debrief on what had happened, and then proceeded back to Tabuk."

PHENOMENAL MAINTENANCE AND GOOD FORTUNE

Discussing the air-to-air victories scored by F-15 pilots that served with the 33rd Tactical Fighter Wing during Desert Storm, Cesar said: "The real success story in Desert Storm, besides having air-to-air kills, was our maintenance teams who did a phenomenal job. We flew the highest number of sorties and flew the highest number of hours of any F-15 unit that flew in combat. We also had the

Five F-15C Eagles assigned to the 58th Tactical Fighter Squadron taxi to the runway at Eglin Air Force Base, Florida for the 20-plus hour flight to Dharan Air Base, Saudi Arabia for Operation Desert Shield. US Air Force

"The missiles launched by me and Chemo both hit the nose of each aeroplane, both exploded into fireballs and totally obliterated each MiG-23."

ighest functional mission capable rate, 98% or our combat window, metrics that were all nade possible by the team effort between ps, maintenance, and security forces. There vere so many great Eagle keeper leaders n our team that it was epic. They had jets eady every day. The weapons troops did verything they could to make sure all our veapons were fully functional. Consequently, ve launched the highest number of missiles nd had the highest number of missile-kills of ny squadron in Desert Storm, even though ther squadrons attempted missile shots. hat's a tribute to the professionalism of ur maintenance and weapons troops who outinely downloaded, uploaded, and BIT-ested missiles.

"In the early days of the war all the F-15 nits were initially assigned specific lanes f responsibility and areas of responsibility, vith the expectation that these weren't going o be swapped around. After about the sixth ay all the activity was in the central and vestern parts of the AOR, and the Langley eam requested they move to the west, and we nove to the east. We weren't there to argue and took the eastern CAPs, Langley took the western CAPs. Well guess what? We got kills in the eastern CAPs, while the Langley team got no kills in the western CAPs, so good fortune played a role.

"Furthermore, squadron training, discipline in the cockpit, discipline of the maintenance teams all mattered to the point that when we faced Iraqi MiGs, we executed to near perfection. We could have always executed better because the heat of battle plays out such that some little things may or may not have been done. We always debriefed those kinds of things. But the truth was, when we were faced with our enemy, we did more of the right things than other squadrons did. We wrote our own chapters of aviation history through teamwork, camaraderie, and the support given to our families back at Eglin.

"We also had the privilege of flying the latest F-15s in the US Air Force inventory laced with technology that gave us unique advantages over other F-15 teams in the region. Of course, we had members of the 58th, 59th, and 60th Tactical Fighter Squadrons in our formations so, we were a group of Nomads, but we always flew with the Gorilla flag when we went to war."

A JOURNEY TO LAKENHEATH

When Cesar's tour with the 58th Tactical Fighter Squadron finished, he was assigned to the 9th Air Force at Shaw Air Force Base, South Carolina as the chief of air-to-air STANEVAL [Standards and Evaluation]. He continued to fly the F-15 both as an instructor and as an evaluator with the active-duty 33rd Tactical Fighter Wing based at Eglin and the 1st Fighter Wing based at Langley. But he also flew with the Air National Guard, specifically Louisiana's 159th Fighter Wing at New Orleans, Georgia's 128th Fighter Wing at Dobbins and Massachusetts' 104th Fighter Wing at Barnes.

Fondly recalling flying with the Air National Guard, Cesar said: "I had to re-learn the systems of the older aeroplanes and understand the differences in culture between an Air National Guard unit and an active-duty unit. Post Desert Storm, some guard units were upgrading to the F-15 and hired a lot of the Desert Storm veterans, old friends

of mine with a lot of experience, so from my perspective, for check rides or flying as an instructor pilot, I didn't have to look at anything other than flying performance, and that made my job very rewarding, and a lot of fun too."

After his STANEVAL tour, Cesar attended the Air Command and Staff College at Maxwell Air Force Base, Alabama, then the Joint Force Staff College in Norfolk, Virginia, then to NATO to work at AIRCENT as the director of the then new Partnership for Peace programme. Cesar was then appointed as the executive officer to Commander United States Air Forces in Europe, General Mike Ryan, and then he was selected by a return to flying board for assignment to RAF Lakenheath, England to serve as the 48th Fighter Wing's chief of safety.

Discussing his assignment to Lakenheath, Cesar said: "In late 1997, I arrived at RAF Lakenheath to join the 48th Fighter Wing, which was my first assignment in Europe to fly with the 493rd Fighter Squadron 'Grim Reapers'. The squadron gave me some great opportunities to fly and re-qualify as a flight lead, mission commander, and instructor pilot, flying the most lethal aeroplane in the world, and training with all the NATO partners that would come up and fly against us. One thing I hated more than anything else about flying from Lakenheath was for almost 11 months out of the year we had to wear poopy suits because of the temperature of the sea, but it was a minor nuisance, and I would trade that any day, just to keep flying."

The two 33rd Tactical Fighter Wing flagship F-15C Eagles in formation flight with a Royal Saudi Air Force F-5 Tiger over the canyon lands of the Saudi desert. US Air Force

OPERATION ALLIED FORCE

The 48th Fighter Wing was heavily involved with NATO's aerial bombing campaign against the Federal Republic of Yugoslavia during the Kosovo War under Operation Allied Force. F-15E Strike Eagles and F-15C Eagles assigned to the 48th flew hundreds combat missions during the campaign and Cesar was one of the F-15C pilots involved. Discussing the operations of the 493rd Fighter Squadron, Cesar said: "For Operation Allied Force, we were lucky enough to not deploy to what we referred to as the USS Aviano. We went to Cervia Air Base, Italy, about 50 miles south of Aviano and had the base pretty much all to ourselves. During the build-up phase we deployed to Cervia for four weeks and returned to Lakenheath. In December [1998], we received a dozen new graduate pilots from the F-15 FTU programme, so we were trying to quickly get them through their mission ready qualifications, but by the time we got the first marching order, they said, 'hey, you guys need to deploy and deploy with what you got'. We also had half the squadron deployed at Incirlik Air Base, Turkey flying missions over northern Iraq enforcing the no-fly zone in support of Operation Northern Watch. When we deployed to Cervia, we had to ask NATO's joint force air component commander, Lieutenant General Michael Short, permission to download some of the jets of missiles so that we could continue mission qualification training. We got them all qualified before the start of the war on March 24.

"We manned alert and DCA HVA CAPs as required and remained the only air dominance assets in the entire AOR for Operation Allied Force and were very much in high demand. We were granted permission from the commander of US Central Command to re-deploy our jets at Incirlik to Cervia, so we were equipped with at least 28 jets with which to fight a full-up war.

Ground crew communicate with the pilots of the 58th Tactical Fighter Squadron before take-off from Eglin Air Force Base, Florida bound for Dharan Air Base, Saudi Arabia in support of Operation Desert Shield. US Air Force

"But the truth was, when we were faced with our enemy, we did more of the right things than other squadrons did."

The aircraft arrived from Incirlik about a week and a half before the war started. We also had to man positions at the CAOC because there was no F-15 expertise there at the time, so as a single F-15 squadron, we were maxed out."

MIG SHOOTDOWN

On the morning of March 23, the 493rd Fighter Squadron received the ATO for the start of the air war the following night. Squadron pilots had undertaken mission planning for a while, had seen prelims of the mission packages, and spoken with the mission commanders for the first three days of the war. They were well prepared and ready to go.

Discussing the squadron's first mission, Cesar said: "Our intelligence personnel informed us of the movement of assets around the country, mostly MiG-29s, in the case of four jets, no details were known of their whereabouts. We had a couple of plans to deal with the Serbian air threat, one included the MiG-29s, so we planned our tactics around the potential that there would be MiG-29s in the area.

"We took off and headed south to the southern edge of the boot of Italy. It was a moonless night, very dark, Italy was lit up in all its grandeur but everything to the east of the Adriatic was pitch black. You could see campfires in different places, but no lights, you could tell it was a suppressed environment. We turned to the north, the strikers stayed with their tanker, and we prepared to start our prestrike sweep. Tony 'K Bob' Sweeney flew the far western F-15, he was number two, just to the east of him was Robert 'Cricket' Renner. He was a recent graduate of the weapons school, and the flight lead for the mission. I was just to the east of Cricket, and then further east of me was 'Wild' Bill Denham, who was one of new guys who had just shown up, with about 70 hours in the F-15, and he's flying his first combat sortie on night one.

"As we headed north, we picked up an initial contact over the Adriatic which was Cricket's responsibility. The target turned out to be a small private aircraft that landed at an airfield in Montenegro which happened to be one of the first targets struck by NATO that night, so who knows how the pilot fared.

"Bill and I had the responsibility of looking over land, Bill had the high look, and as I was monitoring the low look. I started to pick up intermittent hits in between the mountain ranges, but I couldn't really lock on to it, just because the target was flying through valleys. When he got to a point 30 to 40 miles north of Pristina he started climbing in a left-hand turn. I was only able to detect and lock him at 12,000 feet at about 60 to 70 miles and started an ID matrix. Wild Bill and I shared the responsibility of monitoring the target, while looking high and low, respectively. The target continued toward us and climbed to about 14,000 feet. He was on a snap vector directly at the front edge of the strike package, which was about 50 miles behind us. So, it was very clear that his GCI controller was vectoring him to the strike package and didn't see Bill and I at 35,000 feet.

"We completed the ID matrix, just a little bit short of me taking a shot, when our radar warning receivers detected the search radars of Serbian surface-to-air missile [SAM] systems that were locking us up into a full target track mode. So, I directed Wild

An F-15C Eagle loaded with live AIM-9 Sidewinder and AIM-7 Sparrow missiles flies behind a KC-135 tanker over the Saudi Arabian desert during Operation Desert Shield. US Air Force

Bill to head west to stiff-arm the SAMs, completed an ID confirmation, which re-confirmed that the target was a MiG-29 and then shot a single AMRAAM from 35,000 feet, at about Mach 1.3. The missile separated from the underwing pylon, entered a nose-up climb as per its expected profile, got to a higher altitude, and descended toward the target under the guidance of its own radar looking at a focused piece of sky, to find the target.

"At 15 miles range, with six seconds of flight remaining, I checked for any flashing electronic attack indicators, nothing was happening, then looked outside to my right two o'clock position to see a fireball. It was the MiG-29. We subsequently found out that my AMRAAM hit the MiG-29 pretty much directly behind the cockpit. Other pilots reported seeing the fireball from 100 miles away to the south. That was the first kill of Operation Allied Force, which happened not four minutes into what was supposed to be a 50-minute vul period. We were very conscientious of both our gas status and our weapons load out because we didn't know how the vul period would play out. When the last strikers were on the target, there were no tankers near us, though we weren't scheduled to refuel on the way home, so we did the standard F-15 drill, slowly climbed to 45,000 feet, and sauntered our way towards Cervia.

"Mike Shower shot down a MiG-29 to the north of Belgrade early that morning and a Dutch F-16 pilot scored the third kill of the night, the first for a NATO partner. Several days later, Jeff Hwang, from our squadron, scored the first ever track-while-scan double MiG kill from a single sortie, subsequently, an F-16 from Aviano scored the sixth MiG-29 kill of the war."

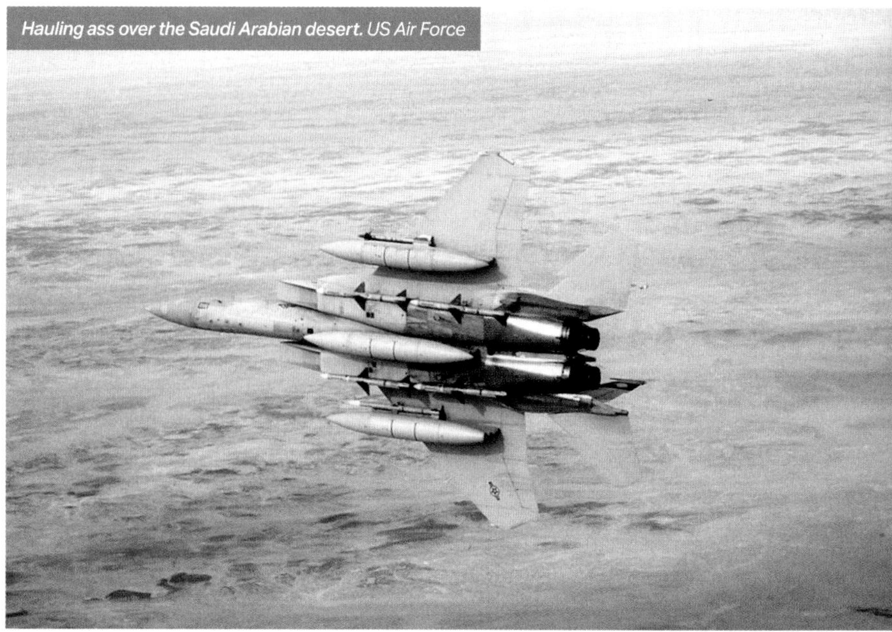
Hauling ass over the Saudi Arabian desert. US Air Force

COMBAT COMPARISON

Having flown combat missions in two operations, Desert Storm in 1991 and Allied Force in 1999, and scored air-to-air victories in both. Discussing the differences between them and the lessons learnt, Cesar said: "Going into Desert Storm, we had the benefit of being able to look at the debriefs from Vietnam. We had created training events like Red Flag in which the objective was to deliver unwavering, persistent air dominance anywhere around the world. When we came out of Desert Storm, there were many lessons learned that were evaluated and incorporated into our ongoing training. We also introduced

During Operation Desert Shield, the 58th Tactical Fighter Squadron flew dissimilar air combat training sorties with Royal Saudi Air Force F-5 Tigers. US Air Force

A crew chief assists Captain Cesar Rodriguez with his seat straps prior to a mission at Eglin Air Force Base, Florida. US Air Force via Cesar Rodriguez

> **"We subsequently found out that my AMRAAM hit the MiG-29 pretty much directly behind the cockpit."**

"When my tour with the 493rd Fighter Squadron at Lakenheath finished, I was assigned to the 1st Fighter Wing based at Langley Air Force Base, Virginia to be the chief of flight safety. I was promoted to colonel, had the privilege to go to the Naval War College in Newport, Rhode Island for a year, then Mountain Home Air Force Base, Idaho, as the deputy commander of the 366th Operations Group under then Colonel Dave Goldfein who later became the Air Force Chief of Staff. During that assignment, General Mosley selected me to spend several months at Tonopah, Nevada, to prepare for what eventually became Operation Iraqi Freedom, then I deployed to Al Jaber Air Base, Kuwait, as the 332nd Expeditionary Operations Group commander before the start of Operation Iraqi Freedom.

"Upon my return to Mountain Home, I was selected to be the 355th Mission Support Group commander at Davis Monthan Air Force Base in Tucson, Arizona. Before I moved to Tucson, I flew the F-15 for about six more months and completed the tour with my fini-flight. I got to fly with the youngest pilot in our squadron. It involved the two of us against four other F-15s and four F-16s. I limited all of them to guns only, so my wingman and I were able to take some pre-merge shots and shoot down some of those guys. We ended up in two separate 1v1 engagements, so it was a great day. At the end of my fini-flight, I had a little under 1,700 hours in the F-15, a little under 900 hours in the A-10 and 800 hours in the AT-38."

the AIM-120 AMRAAM missile which had its flaws, but the concept of a launch and leave missile against the potential foe that would put up more aircraft than we could handle on a particular merge, was exactly what we needed. Other examples of adopting new technology and therefore systems were night-vision goggles and the AIM-9X Sidewinder. Each system has been of great benefit to our pilots.

"Those pilots who fought in Desert Storm asked the Combat Air Force to extend the training provided by the various flying training units from preparing a young pilot to be a safe wingman ready to go into MQT at a fighter squadron to training that got them through MQT so they could fly in a four-ship on their first day at a fighter squadron, ready go to war. That way, all the fighter squadron would need to provide was a local area familiarisation flight. This was adopted and subsequently the new wingmen assigned to the 493rd Fighter Squadron in support of Allied Force were ten times better prepared than I was when I arrived at Eglin for my MQT. They were ready to go to war on day one, and they proved it. Today, our forces continue to become more lethal than those that went before them.

The pilots of the 493rd Fighter Squadron four-ship which shot down two Serbian MiG-29s on March 24, 1999, the first night of Operation Allied Force (L to R) Cesar 'Rico' Rodriguez, Anthony 'K Bob' Sweeney, 'Wild' Bill Denham and Robert 'Cricket' Renner in the squadron building at Cervia Air Base. US Air Force via Cesar Rodriguez

F-15 Ops in Desert Shield and Desert Storm

Despite attending the Air Force Academy, finishing second in his pilot training class, and missing out on an F-15 slot, Don Schilpp went on to qualify as an F-15 pilot in 1988.

F-15C Eagles assigned to the 27th Tactical Fighter Squadron at Dharan Air Base, Saudi Arabia during Operation Desert Focus. US Air Force/SrA Richard Helleman

After graduating from pilot training with the 14th Flying Training Wing based at Columbus Air Force Base, Mississippi, Don Schilpp was selected to become a First Assignment Instructor Pilot (FAIP) for a four-year tour.

Don had wanted to fly the F-15 from the age of 13 after he read about the aircraft in *Reader's Digest* and subsequently seeing a YF-15 prototype flying near St Louis-Lambert Field while his dad was driving them to their vacation location. He told his dad that one day he was going to the Air Force Academy and would one day fly the F-15.

At the end of his first assignment as an instructor pilot in 1987, Don's squadron commander conceded that the air force had screwed him over by making his first assignment an instructor pilot. Don's commander asked him what his first choice was. "F-15," Don replied. He asked Don to fill out the necessary papers which were submitted to the selection board and resulted in Don being selected for the F-15 Eagle.

"Don had wanted to fly the F-15 from the age of 13 after he read about the aircraft in Reader's Digest"

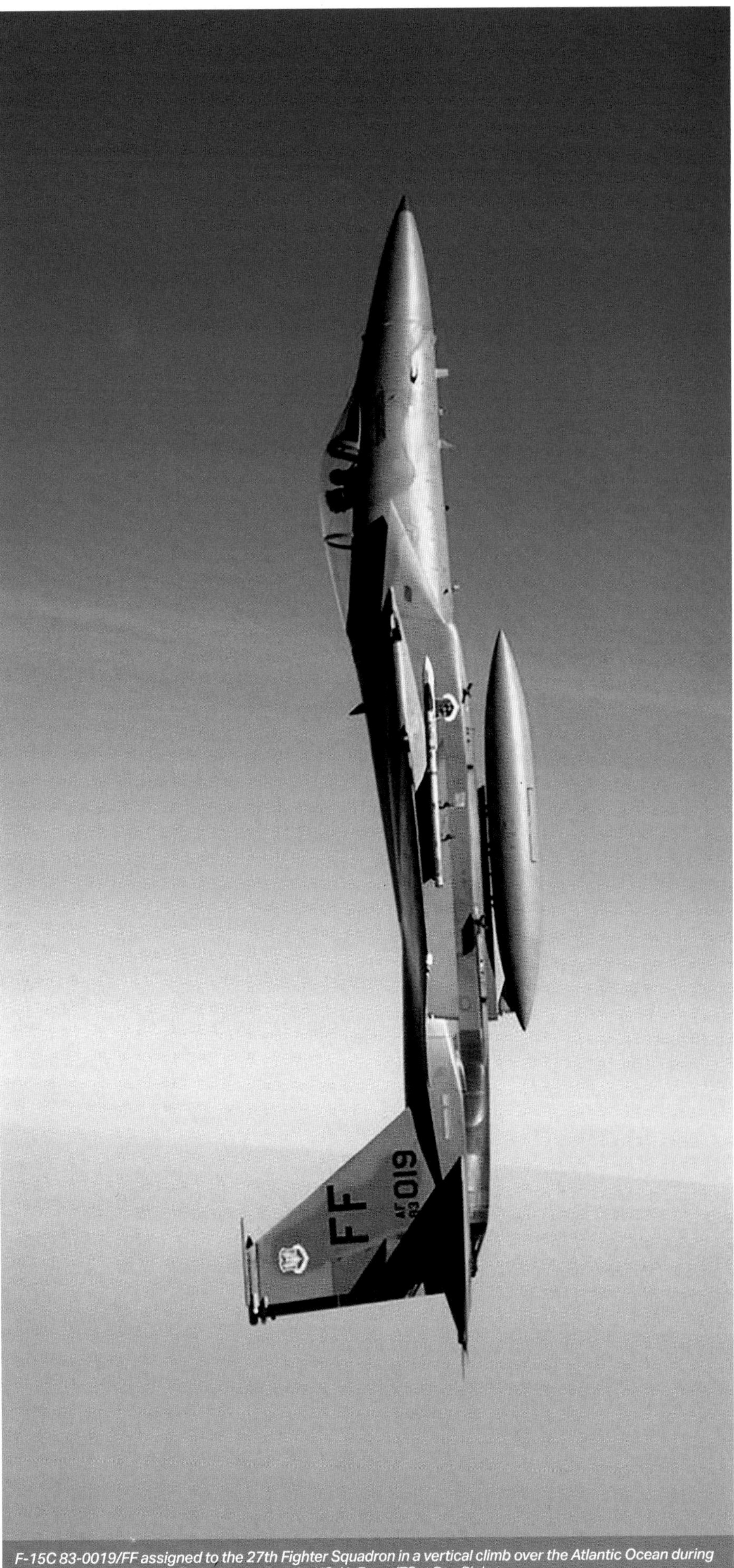

F-15C 83-0019/FF assigned to the 27th Fighter Squadron in a vertical climb over the Atlantic Ocean during a flight from Langley Air Force Base, Virginia. US Air Force/TSgt Ben Bloker

In August 1987, Don was assigned to the 325th Tactical Fighter Wing based at Tyndall Air Force Base, Florida where he took the F-15 B-course with the 1st Tactical Fighter Training Squadron 'Miss Fury'/'Griffins'. After graduating near the top of his class, Don was assigned to the 1st Tactical Fighter Wing based at Langley Air Force Base, Virginia and served with the 27th Tactical Fighter Squadron 'Fightin' Eagles' between May 1988-June 1991.

Don was the flight lead of the second wave of F-15s deployed to Dhahran Air Base in Saudi Arabia for Operation Desert Shield. Recalling the deployment, he said: "Our deployment flight from Langley direct to Dhahran lasted 14 hours with multiple aerial refuellings. It took the 1st Fighter Wing just a few days to generate two squadrons of 24 aeroplanes, the 71st Tactical Fighter Squadron deployed on the first day, the 27th followed on day two. One notable event was getting the Saudis up on the radio as we entered Saudi air space, which was a strange and unusual experience.

"After landing I wondered if there was going to be any shooting or Scud attacks and noticed Hawk trainers parked on ramp. As we were climbing out of our jets a Saudi Hawk buzzed us not 50 feet off the deck, likely a welcome for us, which scared the living crap out of us. We needed some assistance to get out of the cockpit, my ass felt like it would never recover, it was numb, and my body hurt."

"We needed some assistance to get out of the cockpit, my ass felt like it would never recover, it was numb, and my body hurt."

DESERT SHIELD AND DESERT STORM

Describing some of the most notable missions flown from Dharan during both phases of the deployment, Don said: "The closest I ever came to shooting somebody down was on my first mission of Desert Shield. We were flying a CAP in the area along the southern Saudi-Kuwait border when I locked up a MiG-23 at a range of probably 25 miles. I expected the Iraqi pilot to turn because we were both headed toward the border. When I saw an AWACS flying above me, just 15 miles from the MiG while hauling ass toward the border, I referred to my knee pad to get the code word for the AWACS. The word was retrograde, which I screamed out on the radio to warn the AWACS pilot, but he was not responding so I switched to the guard frequency, screamed the code word again which gained his attention. He immediately turned away from the border as I held my radar locked on to the MiG because the pilot was clearly going after the AWACS. At about the 10-mile range, my finger was on the pickle button ready to shoot the MiG, but the rules of engagement deemed any wreckage had to fall to earth on the Saudi Arabian side of the border. Closing fast, the MiG and me were both positioned about two miles either side of the border. At the point I was about to fire, the MiG pilot pulled a high-g left turn and headed back north. That was the closest I came to killing somebody. Part of me wished that I had killed a MiG, but I was glad that I did not for fear that the wreckage would have landed in Kuwait for which I would have received a month long, expenses paid vacation in Diego Garcia, in other words jail.

"My scariest mission was during Desert Shield. The war hadn't kicked off and we were not supposed to go into Iraqi territory. My squadron commander had flown the mission before us, and we were lucky enough to talk to him before we got airborne. He said, be careful there are MiG-25s airborne and they are flying in flights of three [our intelligence had always stated there would be two aircraft] Well during our mission, we encountered three MiG-25s and I had a difficult time convincing our intelligence personnel and some pilots that the Iraqis were operating flights of three aircraft, but we figured it out, and alerted all the other F-15 units. I advised them the Iraqis were operating like that on purpose to make us think they were operating flights of two aircraft, not three. The third aircraft was trying to get in and attack the AWACS. That was a very challenging mission. Even after the war, some fellow war veterans still questioned my story.

"During Desert Storm we flew a CAP [combat air patrol] mission which involved going to a tanker and then head north to fly a big circle around Baghdad, the area that US Air Force F-15s shot down some Iraqi MiGs and Mirages when the aircraft tried to escape to the east and fly to Iran. Those missions generally lasted for at least ten hours.

"On another CAP, my wingman and I had a wake-up call when an F/A-18 flying from the south shot a HARM missile [an AGM-88 High-speed Anti-Radiation Missile] between us: we had a chuckle and laugh about that later. I felt a little scared on my first couple of missions, but because I'd trained and prepared for it during my whole career, I felt thoroughly in my element, and that the F-15 was the best.

"We escorted every type of aircraft during the war, on one mission there were 120 strike

Two F-15C Eagles assigned to the 94th Tactical Fighter Squadron take-off from Langley Air Force Base in June 1989. US Air Force/MSgt William Belcher

F-15C Eagles on the end of runway ramp at a base in US Central Command's area of responsibility. US Air Force/SrA Manuel Martinez

aircraft behind my four-ship. Turned out the primary target was occluded by weather. Turning 120 aircraft around to head for the secondary target in front of the weather and a large thunderstorm was interesting. They were amazing missions, thinking back about how many aircraft were in the air, how many tankers were in the air, hundreds, and hundreds of aircraft airborne at any given time, with just about everybody following the rules. That said, I remember a four-ship of F-111s flying right in front of my tanker and right over the top one of my wingmen while we were on the tanker: they clearly weren't following the rules.

"I flew 36 combat missions over the 42 days of the air war, I flew just about every day, averaged about four hours of sleep per day, ate about one meal a day, and lost about 10 pounds of weight. They were long missions that lasted between eight and 12 hours. The deployment was the biggest experience of my career. I felt completely in my element but combat of course is scary. I flew in one of the first daytime missions of the war as the lead of the second four-ship. We were targeted by all kinds of surface-to-air missiles [SAMs] but thank God, we defeated them."

"At the point I was about to fire, the MiG pilot pulled a high-g left turn and headed back north. That was the closest I came to killing somebody."

TYNDALL, LANGLEY, AND KEFLAVIK

After returning to Langley, Don completed his tour with the 27th Tactical Fighter Squadron and was then assigned to the 325th Tactical Fighter Wing based at Tyndall Air Force Base, Florida where he became an instructor on a three-year tour, initially with the 95th Fighter Squadron 'Mr Bones'. He then worked at the Pentagon [94-97], initially for the F-22 programme then for the requirements office on what became the Joint

Six F-15C Eagles assigned to the 94th Fighter Squadron taxi to the flight line on their return to Langley Air Force Base after a four-month deployment to Incirlik Air Base, Turkey in support of Operation Northern Watch. US Air Force/SSgt Travis Aston

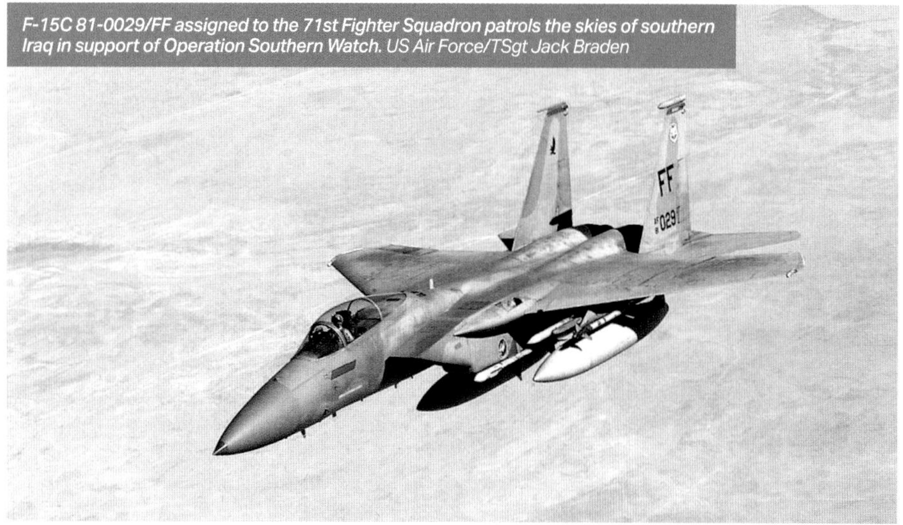

F-15C 81-0029/FF assigned to the 71st Fighter Squadron patrols the skies of southern Iraq in support of Operation Southern Watch. US Air Force/TSgt Jack Braden

"Trying to shoot down a MiG-25 with an AIM-7 Sparrow missile was very difficult. You had to almost make a perfect intercept."

Strike Fighter. After his tour at the Pentagon, Don returned to Langley to serve with the 94th Fighter Squadron 'Spads', by then flying F-15s upgraded to the MSIP standard and armed with AIM-120 AMRAAM missiles. He made two deployments to the Middle East in support of Operation Southern Watch. During those deployments Don got to chase some Iraqi MiG-25s.

Detailing flights during Operation Southern Watch, Don said: "We planned one mission like Operation Bolo in the Vietnam war led by Colonel Robin Olds, commander, 8th Tactical Fighter Wing. Operation Bolo used a deception tactic that lured and trapped North Vietnamese MiG-21s by mimicking an F-105 bombing formation. Use of the tactic during the 12-minute engagement resulted in seven North Vietnamese MiG-21s - about half of thei operational force – being shot down with no US Air Force losses.

"On one mission flown during my second deployment in support of Operation Southern Watch we almost bagged an Iraqi MiG-25. During Operation Desert Storm in 1991, trying to shoot down a MiG-25 with an AIM-7 Sparrow missile was very difficult. You had to almost make a perfect intercept. It didn't concern us, because you knew if you had the awareness and knew of a missile lock-on you could defend yourself from a MiG-25's air-to-air weapons.

The 1st Tactical Fighter Wing F-15C flagship loaded with live fuselage-mounted AIM-7 Sparrow missiles and AIM-9 Sidewinders carried on the wing pylon in June 1983. US Air Force/TSgt Bob Williams

Three F-15C Eagles assigned to the 94th Fighter Squadron armed with AIM-120 AMRAAM missiles and loaded with three external fuel tanks over the North Atlantic during a re-deployment flight back to Langley Air Force Base from the US Central Command theatre. US Air Force/Mark Bucher

"Later during Operation Southern Watch, we were armed with AIM-120 AMRAAM missiles which meant you didn't have to fly a perfect intercept, per se. And of course, the AMRAAM had a lot more capability against a high-flying, fast fighter. The two biggest capabilities you had to watch out for when going after a MiG-25 were altitude and speed. So, we weren't nearly as concerned about the Iraqi MiG-25s during Southern Watch because we were carrying AIM-120 missiles and the F-15's radar and navigation systems had been improved. And of course, the closer we got to catching them, the less likely they were to come up and fly, and when they did come up and fly, they did the bat turn from hell and got out of dodge much faster and much sooner."

Toward the end of his tour with the 94th Fighter Squadron, Keflavik, Iceland was the location for one interesting deployment. The squadron detachment was tasked to air police Icelandic airspace checking out the occasional Russian Air Force Tu-95 *Bear* bomber flying in the region on a mission from Engels, Shaykovka, and Soltsy Air Bases.

In 2000, Don returned to the Pentagon for his final four years in the US Air Force. He was at work in the Pentagon when the building was attacked on 9/11, two sides away from the crash site. Concluding his story of that terrible day, Don said: "Ironically, I was in office number 5d, 911, how's that for a crazy coincidence?"

A line of F-15C Eagles assigned to the 94th Fighter Squadron 'Spads' at Langley Air Force Base during an operational readiness inspection. Thirty-four aircraft were generated to demonstrate the 1st Fighter Wing's ability to prepare and deploy personnel, equipment and support assets to a combat environment. US Air Force/TSgt Ben Bloker

Bulldogs and

Dale Mancuso was an F-15C pilot who flew the aircraft in the United States, Europe, and in combat in the Middle East.

Dale Mancuso completed pilot training in 1985 and was selected for the F-15 Eagle. He was assigned to Luke Air Force Base, Arizona and the 58th Tactical Training Wing, and learnt to fly the Eagle with the 461st Tactical Tighter Training Squadron 'Deadly Jesters'.

Discussing his class and the changes compared to his pilot training, Dale said: "There were five students in my class supervised by as many instructors. The change in mentality was an eye-opener, during flying training you were on a squadron with students from all walks of life who would ultimately serve in different types of combat aircraft, at Luke, just fighter pilots manned the squadron. The course was demanding.

"At the end of my course, I was selected for an assignment with the 21st Tactical Fighter Wong based at Elmendorf Air Force Base, Alaska. Another pilot selected for an assignment with the 36th Tactical Fighter Wing based at Bitburg Air Base, didn't want to go to West Germany. Fortunately, we were able to switch at the last minute which was a huge change for me."

BECOMING A BULLDOG

When Dale arrived at Bitburg he was assigned to the 525th Tactical Fighter Squadron 'Bulldogs' which had the primary task of defending West German airspace with F-15 aircraft sat on alert. Discussing flight operations with the squadron, Dale said: "My first task with the squadron was to complete mission ready training, a 20-flight programme to learn the mission and the tactics used by the squadron. This involved learning about all the different

Fightin' Eagles

Dale Mancuso's first operational F-15 unit was the 525th Tactical Fighter Squadron 'Bulldogs' based at Bitburg Air Base, West Germany. One of the squadron's aircraft, F-15C 79-0058/BT seen over West Germany loaded with AIM-7 Sparrow (on the fuselage pylons) and AIM-9 Sidewinder (underwing pylons) missiles. US Air Force

rules until the squadron felt you were mission ready. Once you were declared mission ready, you started sitting alert, dubbed Zulu alert, 24-hours a day, which required you to be airborne in five minutes even from a dead sleep.

"We practiced a lot of low-level missions using free flight, a system that allowed all fighters from all countries to fly around below 10,000ft pretty much anywhere except the restricted areas. Many of the aircraft using West German airspace were strike aircraft flying on low-level routes. Tasked with air defence, we cruised around trying to locate and simulate attacks on them."

Each of the three fighter squadrons based at Bitburg maintained alert, each taking its turn in accordance with the roster. Often East German aircraft would approach the border and turn away at the last minute. In response, the alert jets at Bitburg were scrambled to head for the border only to be called back when the East German aircraft turned away. Commenting on the task, Dale said: "All alert scrambles had a heightened sense of anticipation from the start. Getting airborne in five minutes was a huge deal especially in the middle of the night, you went from being sound asleep to taking off in an F-15, often in bad weather. We took off to the west, immediately pulled a 4g or 5g turn to head back to the east and the border.

"In general, you had a feel for the political spectrum, and if there wasn't anything going on politically, then to me there was a little less anticipation of something real happening. Had there been more heightened political activity, then it would certainly have been different. Periodically there were days when you would practice no communication launches and quick turns. You would fly a mission with a specific responsibility, you'd return to Bitburg, go to the fuel pit, and with one engine running, you'd get refuelled and go out again. You'd repeat that process three times in a day."

EUROPEAN MISSIONS

United States Air Forces Europe served, and still serves, the entire European continent

"At Luke [AFB], just fighter pilots manned the squadron. The course was demanding."

which meant that it's fighter squadrons and their pilots flew in all the European countries, from northern Norway to southern Turkey. Providing some examples, Dale said: "We regularly deployed to Decimomannu Air Base on the island of Sardinia and made regular two-week detachments to Denmark, Norway, and Spain for exercises and air combat training. Most of these events were conducted for familiarisation with airspace and the terrain. At weekends we often flew around Europe, maybe RAF Alconbury or RAF Lakenheath in England, stay overnight, fly air combat training missions on the Saturday and then fly to Torrejon Air Base, Spain on the Sunday, once again stay overnight, fly to Aviano on the Monday, and finally return to Bitburg. We accomplished a lot of flying over the course of such a weekend and met different training requirements.

"On one four-ship mission from Bitburg a huge weather pattern closed in across West Germany creating near-zero visibility which caused airports to close. We were given Cologne as a diversion airfield but when we got down to our minimums, the runway was not visible, and back then we couldn't land

F-15C 82-0023/FF assigned to the 27th Tactical Fighter Squadron based at Langley Air Force Base, Virginia in a steep climb. US Air Force/MSgt Herbert Cintron Jr

F-15C Eagles parked outside the Roether Memorial Zulu Alert Facility at Bitburg Air Base, West Germany. US Air Force

> "Once you were declared mission ready, you started sitting alert, dubbed Zulu alert, 24-hours a day, which required you to be airborne in five minutes even from a dead sleep."

with zero visibility. So, we climbed out in trail, and were heading to the North Sea to eject because we had no other choice, but when over Belgium there was an area where we could see through the clouds, so we descended, spotted a runway, didn't know what airport it was, and landed there and were very happy about that. Turned out it was a Belgian military base.

"When we were deployed to Bodø in Northern Norway, we flew north over the ocean to check out Soviet warships and on one mission saw Tu-95 *Bear* bombers flying in an area to the north of Bodø."

FIGHTING EAGLES AND WEAPONS SCHOOL

At the completion of his tour at Bitburg, Dale was assigned to the 1st Tactical Fighter Wing based at Langley Air Force Base, Virginia and served with the 27th Tactical Fighter Squadron 'Fightin' Eagles'. The unit was the first US Air Force squadron to operate the F-15 Eagle, the first F-15A model assigned to the 27th arrived at Langley in January 1976. Today's F-22-equipped 27th Fighter Squadron is now in its 128th year, it was formed at Kelly Field, Texas as the 27th Aero Squadron on May 8, 1917.

During his time with the 27th Tactical Fighter Squadron, Dale was selected to attend the US Air Force Fighter Weapons School at Nellis Air Force Base, Nevada. Commenting on the six-month course, he said: "It was an intense programme which required lots of mission planning and preparation. You would prepare for one mission over three or four days, almost all day and all night. There was no limitation, no corners were cut, so you spent hours or days preparing for your briefing and your mission, and you were expected to maintain a social presence.

"The syllabus involved various scenarios, 1 v 1, 1 v 2, 2 v 2, that you had to go through. You prepared and briefed your mission to a panel of instructors, who were all weapons officers with extremely high standards. So, if you messed anything up, you knew, you weren't going to pass that ride. It was a drain, it was very intense that required not just flying skills, but leadership, briefing and teaching skills.

"The course was about learning and teaching the F-15 tactics. You had to perform, and you had to teach, and you had to do it all together.

There was no slack. You couldn't do this well, and that not well, everything had to be perfect. The school's instructors flew with you in other aircraft, and they had to meet the demands of the challenges of each mission, so when we all got back to Nellis everybody, students and instructors were sweating. Then the debrief started: one I attended lasted for 15 hours.

"I remember a large force exercise mission in an eastern area of the Nellis range which used all altitude blocks [up to 50,000 feet]. It was intense, involved multiple engagements with the aggressor F-16s. I took some kill shots and had to descend to a couple of hundred feet to egress and re-join with the rest of the aircraft in my force. I remember feeling lucky that I didn't hit anybody because there were jets all over the place, just remarkable. It was a feeling of holy cow! But mission success was the focus so you couldn't cut a corner or call a timeout. You just had to do what you had to do and survive.

"When you completed the course, it was a such a relief, you felt like you were at the highest standard that you could ever be at. You felt like there was nothing you hadn't done or mastered, but of course you had to work very hard to get there. I graduated in 1989.

"When I returned to the 27th Tactical Fighter Squadron, I didn't walk right into the weapons officer job because there was already a weapons officer on the squadron, so we worked together during my transition to me being the weapons officer. I took a supervisory role in the vault, the place we kept the classified documents and where a lot of classified training occurred. After a month or so I became the squadron weapons officer, and the previous weapons officer became a flight commander.

"When you come out of a military school, you're very regimented so you need to lighten up a little bit. You're not dealing with the same level of expertise on your squadron. You must adjust to that, gain perspective, and not expect everyone to perform like you when you were at the weapons school."

DESERT STORM

Dale's graduation from the weapons school coincided with the beginning of Operation Desert Shield which required the squadron to deploy to Saudi Arabia. Recalling the deployment, he said: "We deployed, and our aircraft were the first US Air Force fighter aircraft to arrive in the kingdom at a time when there were very few US ground forces deployed. If the Iraqis crossed the border, our plan was to fly as far south as we could go and eject. It was probably a five-hour drive from the Kuwaiti border to Dharan in a tank! As US ground forces continued to arrive in theatre over time, our situation somewhat normalised.

"In general, you had a feel for the political spectrum, and if there wasn't anything going on politically, then to me there was a little less anticipation of something real happening."

"We created missions with target zones and battle plans for how we would interact with the other aircraft types in theatre, how we would identify each other and made sure all the pilots were qualified and understood the rules of engagement. It was a busy time, and it was new, so we were figuring it out as we went, but we had plenty of time to get ready.

"Prior to the start of Operation Desert Storm, I was reassigned to Bitburg, this time with the 53rd Tactical Fighter Squadron 'Tiger', but I didn't want to leave Dharan right away. I was torn between leaving and not leaving Saudi Arabia, consequently I lost my slot at the 53rd, which was taken by Thomas Dietz, who ended up shooting down three Iraqi aircraft, two MiG-21s and a Su-22, so that would have been my slot. My move to Bitburg did come and I was subsequently assigned to the 22nd Tactical Fighter Squadron 'Stingers'.

"Pilots assigned to the 22nd Tactical Fighter Squadron were split between the 525th Tactical Fighter Squadron 'Bulldogs' at Incirlik Air Base, Turkey and the 53rd Tactical Fighter Squadron at Al Kharj, Saudi Arabia.

"At the start of Desert Storm, we flew sweep missions, but we soon owned the sky such that our tasking was changed to air defence,

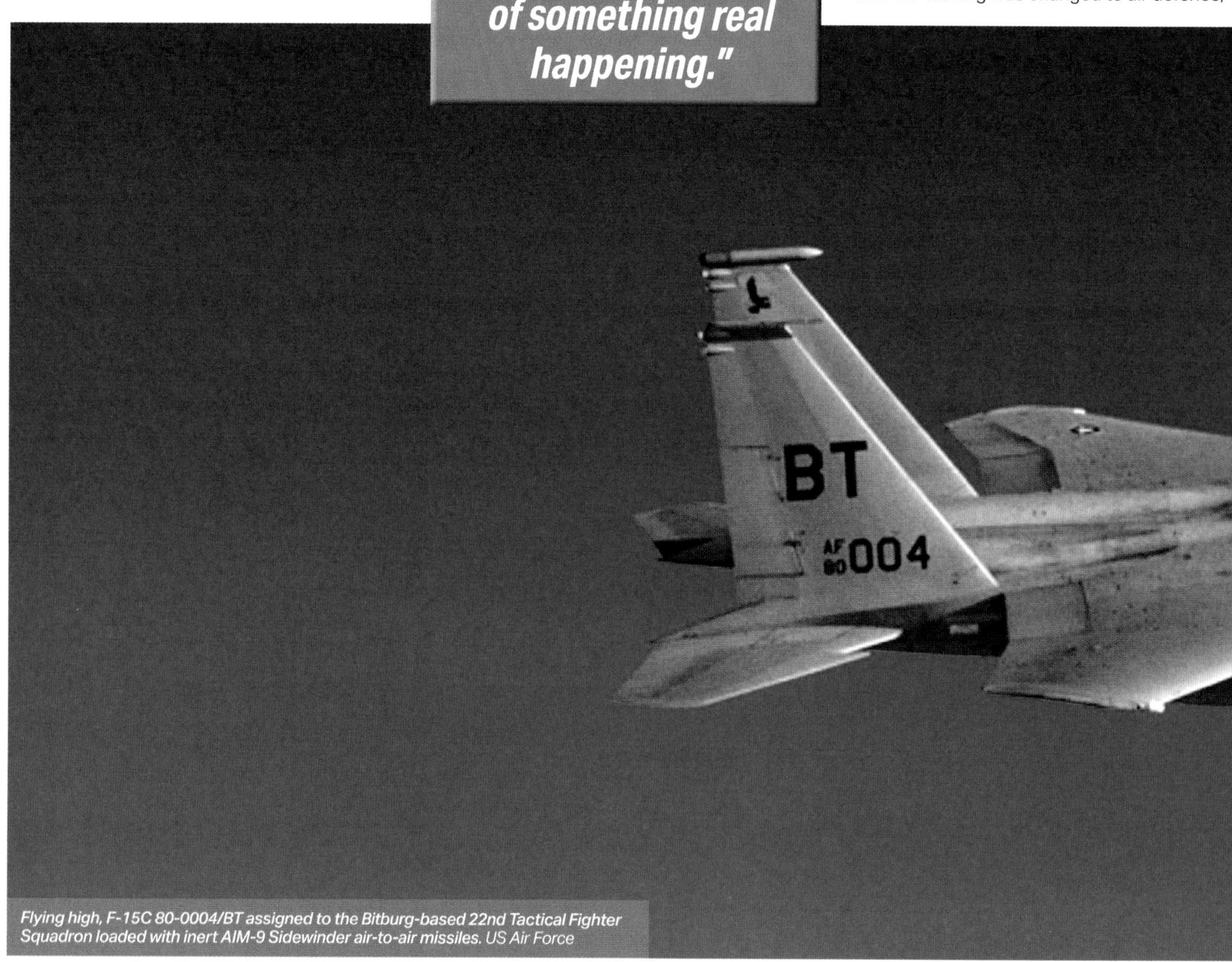

Flying high, F-15C 80-0004/BT assigned to the Bitburg-based 22nd Tactical Fighter Squadron loaded with inert AIM-9 Sidewinder air-to-air missiles. US Air Force

A 27th Tactical Fighter Squadron F-15C configured with one external fuel tank on the centreline station, and a single inert captive carriage CATM-120 AMRAAM missile. US Air Force

Dale Mancuso graduated from the US Air Force Weapons School at Nellis Air Force Base, Nevada in 1989. Two F-15C aircraft assigned to the 57th Wing/Weapons School overfly the dramatic landscape of southern Nevada. *US Air Force*

"Consequently I lost my slot at the 53rd, which was taken by Thomas Dietz, who ended up shooting down three Iraqi aircraft, two MiG-21s and a Su-22."

spending up to nine hours on CAP over Iraq. Once the excitement died down, F-15C Eagles were not as critical per se, as the guys that were conducting strike missions. We remained at Al Kharj for a couple of months beyond the cessation of hostilities.

"Toward the end of my Langley assignment, the US Air Force introduced a bonus, where you received another $12,000 a year to stay in, but you had to commit to stay in through to your 13th year. For personal reasons I didn't take

ıe bonus and opted to leave the active-duty ır force in 1993. I subsequently joined the Air orce Reserve and flew the C-5A Galaxy with ıe 709th Airlift Squadron based at Dover Air orce Base, Delaware. At the end of my time ith the Air Force Reserve, I moved to Colorado prings and worked for the Air Force Academy."

RATING THE F-15

ale liked the F-15 from his first flight in the et. Describing the Eagle, he said: "There was nothing like it, it was highly respected and unique with the sole mission of air superiority. For that role, in my opinion there was no comparison, other aeroplanes did things well. In air combat there were times when the F-16 had a slight advantage, but across the board the F-15 was unmatched, whether it was the number of the of missiles it carried, the endurance, the radar, there was nothing lacking.

"The F-15 commanded respect among the other type-communities in US Air Force service for sure. In a Red Flag scenario, the red force always had to fly under the parameters of potential adversary aircraft, so their hands were a little tied. The Eagle has such an advantage that you weren't creating a false situation, you were making it realistic. It achieved 10 to nothing kill ratios, using the parameters we were given. There was no other aeroplane I wanted to switch to."

Williams Air Force Base outside the city of Mesa, Arizona, was closed as a training base in September 1993. Today the airfield is in operation as Phoenix-Mesa Gateway Airport. However, when Tim Shields reported there in 1987 it was home to the 82nd Flying Training Wing. Tim completed his pilot training at Williams in 1988 but missed out on the single F-15 slot offered to his class.

Instead, Tim was one of 17 of his class selected for a First Assignment Instructor Pilot or FAIP slot. Explaining the selection, Tim said: "There were 60 people in my class, so the number of FAIP slots offered was high. Five of us went to a new base to complete our instructor course. My assignment was with the 323rd Flying Training Wing based at Mather Air Force Base, California. I flew the T-37B with student weapon system officers [WSOs], at the time future F-15E and F-111 WSOs, future Tornado crew from Germany and Italy.

"During my three-year tour at Mather, I flew the T-37B trainer aircraft which had about 2,000 pounds of thrust between the two engines before I got my F-15 assignment. At the time there were plenty of FAIPs in the F-15 community." Before starting F-15 training Tim was required to undertake lead-in fighter training, dubbed LIFT,

F-15A Eagles 77-0137/HO (near) and 77-0101/HO assigned to the 7th Tactical Fighter Squadron based at Holloman Air Force Base, New Mexico. As seen, the near aircraft has flag-ship tail markings applied for the squadron commander. US Air Force

A Screaming Demon

Tim Shields served as an F-15 pilot with two wings and deployed to the Netherlands during the Cold War and flew combat missions during Operation Desert Storm.

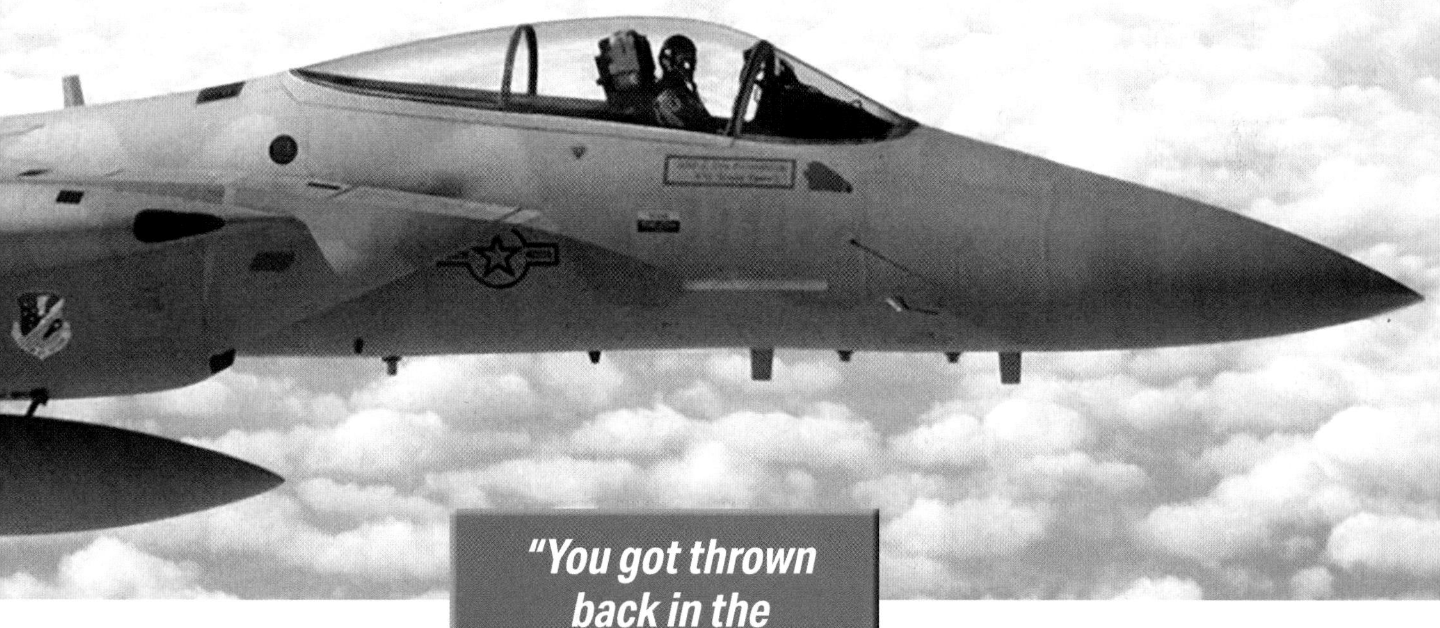

EAD-IN FIGHTER TRAINING

iscussing LIFT training, Tim said: ‸ead-in fighter training was the vital link etween basic flight school and primary 'eapon system training with the 479th actical Training Wing based at Holloman ir Force Base."

IFT was defined by the USAF as: "A natural ansition from learning the basic skills ecessary for a universally assigned pilot to ıe learning of basic fighter pilot skills in the familiar environment of a T-38, the student's last training aircraft."

> **"You got thrown back in the instructor pilot pool and competed with your peers from the other pilot training bases."**

Explaining, Tim said: "The course was designed to transform newly graduated pilots selected to fly fighter aircraft into fighter wingmen by learning, for example, transition, tactical formation flying, basic fighter manoeuvres, air combat manoeuvring and low-level navigation. It lasted 40 days and comprised about 30 hours of flight time."

Tim completed LIFT in 1988 and was assigned to the 405th Tactical Training

Wing based at Luke Air Force Base, Arizona, and learnt how to fly the F-15 with the 555th Tactical Fighter Training Squadron 'Triple Nickel'. He joined the squadron as a brand-new captain with about 1,800 hours of flight time.

Commenting on his assignment to Luke, Tim said: "You got thrown back in the instructor pilot pool once you completed your FAIP tour and then competed with your peers from the other pilot training bases. That was difficult because the 323rd Flying Training Wing was the only navigator training wing and selection was based on your ranking within your class. There were seven F-15 slots up for grabs, and I was fortunate enough to get one.

"My F-15 training class at Luke comprised three captains, six active-duty lieutenants, and one Louisiana Air National Guard lieutenant fresh from pilot training. Students in my class were split between the two F-15 training squadrons. Two of us went to the 555th TFTS 'Triple Nickel', the others went to the 461st TFTS 'Jesters'. The 555th had to wedge our two-person class in to its busy schedule because the 461st was undermanned and only had capacity for eight students at that time.

"My second flight was the zoom ride and was memorable. My instructor pilot was 'Cowboy' Ellis. We were the first take-off of the day, timed for about 15 minutes after sunrise. We were flying an F-15B, the F-15A and F-15B models were susceptible to afterburner blowouts and compressor stalls. Believe it or not, we had a dual compressor stall immediately upon my selection of after burner during the take-off roll. Flames shot out from the huge intakes about 50 feet in front of the aeroplane on both sides. I thought the aircraft had blown up, but Cowboy knew what the problem was, so he put it into idle and rolled out. It was a spectacular event for my second ride in the F-15.

"For my first dissimilar air combat tactics ride, my instructor briefed for a 2 v X but didn't say what the threat was. When we got to the merge in the first engagement, the opposing aircraft were US Marine Corps Kfirs, well, I didn't know the Marines operated Kfirs. My instructor had set up the first engagement as a visual identification engagement, meaning I couldn't shoot until we had visually identified the other aircraft as an enemy. It was surprising to merge with an aircraft that I was unfamiliar with!"

After successful completion of the F-15 B-course at Luke in January 1989, Tim was assigned to the 7th Tactical Fighter Squadron 'Screamin' Demons', a component of the 49th Tactical Fighter Wing based at Holloman Air Force Base, New Mexico, the last F-15A-model wing in the active-duty air force. The F-15A was equipped with the original APG-63 radar, F100 engines, and had no chaff and flare dispensers, a configuration that eventually kept the 49th Tactical Fighter Wing out of Desert Storm.

"The opposing aircraft were US Marine Corps Kfirs, well, I didn't know the Marines operated Kfirs."

Describing his arrival at the 7th Tactical Fighter Squadron, Tim said: "As a brand-new wingman, you go through mission qualification training [MQT], a 12-flight programme to get you up to snuff on employing the aeroplane. That gave me the opportunity to learn how to proficiently use the 11 switches on the stick and 13 on the throttles, playing the piccolo, as they called it. Missions were flown in either four or eight-ships. At that point we were conducting the wall of Eagles concept of employment, flying in line-abreast formation, particularly against F-16s, because the AIM-120 AMRAAM missile was not carried by the F-16 at that time, and the emphasis in MQT was learning how to employ weapons with at an appropriate time.

"The squadron regularly deployed to Nellis Air Force Base, Nevada to support the Fighter Weapons School F-16 squadron flying against some of the best pilots from the F-16 community. We provided dissimilar Red Air to their syllabus. But we had our hands tied, because it was their school, they were paying and it was their rules. Because, at the time, the F-16 didn't have a radar-guided missile threat, the Fighter Weapon School restricted our use of the AIM-7 Sparrow radar-guided missiles quite a bit, otherwise we would have held an advantage."

The fighter squadrons assigned to the 49th Tactical Fighter Wing had a NATO commitment to deploy to and operate from

The F-15's air brake is unmissable when deployed. US Air Force

An early shot of F-15A 77-0099/HO painted with a blue and white chequered tail stripe, the colours of the 7th Tactical Fighter Squadron loaded with an inert AIM-9 Sidewinder and two live AIM-7 Sparrow missiles. US Air Force

forward operating base in Europe to help repel a Soviet invasion through the Fulda Gap. Regular deployments were made under the Chequered Flag programme. During Tim's tour at Holloman his squadron was deployed to Gilze-Rijen Air Base in the Netherlands where he began his flight lead upgrade. That deployment provided him with his first tanker drag, his first transatlantic crossing, his first tactical deployment to another country, and opportunities to fly at low-level within the NATO low-fly system.

Then, in 1990, Iraqi ground forces invaded Kuwait. The United States launched Operation Desert Shield to deter Saddam Hussein from ordering his forces to invade Saudi Arabia. Commenting on the eagerness of the fighter community to deploy in support of Operation Desert Shield, Tim said: "We all wanted to know if we were deploying. People who aren't in the military, don't understand why you want to go to war, you don't want to be left out because you're a swinging-dick fighter pilot! So, it was challenging to not be in the initial rotation. Although we were told we would deploy and were gearing up to deploy before Christmas 1990, the plan got cancelled because our aircraft were not equipped with chaff and flare dispensers for self-defence. So many resources went to the war such that at Holloman I flew about seven hours a month during Desert Shield and Desert Storm. We were having a hard time keeping current in our tanker requirements."

The then Tactical Air Command's Exercise Red Flag held at Nellis Air Force Base,

Formation photo of four F-15A Eagles, one from each of the three squadrons based at Holloman, 7th Tactical Fighter Squadron (near), 8th Tactical Fighter Squadron (middle), 9th Tactical Fighter Squadron (far) and the 49th Tactical Fighter Wing turning away at the top. US Air Force

Nevada was a regular event for the three Holloman-based F-15 squadrons. Detailing some aspects of his own participation in Red Flag, Tim said: "My time at Red Flag was exciting because I finally got upgraded to mission commander, which is always a big deal for any pilot, made better for me because we were flying with NATO allies. Fighting against dedicated aggressor pilots flying F-16s, the wily bandits who know that airspace back and forth was challenging not least because the Red Air force was augmented by F-16s operated by other squadrons. Additionally, the Blue Air force included F-16s, so making sure we weren't going to frat any Blue Air friendly F-16s was a challenge. Aircraft configuration was one way to visually differentiate: aggressor F-16s were fitted with a single external centre line fuel tank while F-16s assigned to Blue Air carried two tanks, one under each wing.

"Prior to take-off for one Red Flag mission, I suffered a maintenance abort while holding on the end of runway ramp. When I cycled my flight controls one last time, my squadron weapons officer, who was upgrading me at the time, and the number three aircraft, asked me to cycle the flight controls again after which he said my aircraft was leaking hydraulic fluid. So, I aborted my mission, and he led the mission with seven rather than eight F-15s. I got to lead a Blue Air mission a couple of days later. The strike

An F-15A assigned to the 7th Tactical Fighter Squadron on the taxiway at Holloman Air Force Base. US Air Force

ackage comprised four A-10s, three B-1Bs, ne E-3, eight F-15s, 34 F-16s, and tankers.

"Desert Shield was going on at the time of is Red Flag, so the threat laydown presented the red force included simulated MiG-29s nd whatever air-to-air and surface-to-air issiles were deemed to be in the Iraqi ventory at the time. Having to defeat such issiles and keep all the strike aircraft together as challenging because Red Flag is as close to combat as you can get without being in a war. But in all honesty, we were short of assets, to only have eight F-15s to cover such a large package of strike aircraft was a little unrealistic, but you had to take what you could get.

"During the missions, the air space was teeming with aeroplanes, they were everywhere, especially once the turning started. It was an all-altitude war, but once you were below 10,000 feet, you were limited to turns of 180°, and had to disengage as a safety limitation. But if you merged with a Red Air F-16 and turned 180°, rocked your wings to say goodbye, the F-16 would still be out there. There was a saying, if you're not cheating, you're not trying, and I think the aggressors at Nellis perfected that, because if you shot one, they didn't always go all the way to their regeneration point to regenerate themselves. But they were limited in their numbers too and

> ***"F-15 pilots were not the greatest for looking out because the aircraft's size made it easier to fly in tactical formation with another aircraft, so we tended to lose sight of something as small as an F-16."***

Tim Shields served as an instructor pilot with the 95th Tactical Fighter Training Squadron 'Mr Bones' at Tyndall Air Force Base, Florida. F-15C 78-0542/TY is shown on take-off from the Florida superbase. US Air Force

wanted to give you as full-up a fight as they could.

"F-15 pilots were not the greatest for looking out because the aircraft's size made it easier to fly in tactical formation with another aircraft, so we tended to lose sight of something as small as an F-16. Red Flag was good for encountering such a scenario and also provided opportunities to fly close to the ground, which we didn't do so much during regular training because we wanted to do basic fighter manoeuvres, which also required a 10,000 foot floor."

When Tim's tour with the 7th Tactical Fighter Squadron finished, he was assigned to the 325th Tactical Fighter Wing based at Tyndall Air Force Base, Florida as an instructor serving with the 95th Tactical Fighter Training Squadron 'Boneheads'. Discussing his instructor upgrade programme, Tim said: "My instructor course at Tyndall was flown in F-15A models. I was excited to get another F-15 assignment, but I wasn't super confident about being an instructor, but the instructor course turned out to be good despite some challenges. I didn't pass every ride, but my flight commander Charly Shugg ensured I met standards.

"I taxied down the long, lonely taxiway out to the boneyard and shut it down with no write ups; it was a great aeroplane, that got chopped up."

"I was the only pilot on my instructor course that had previously flown the F-15A, all my counterparts were already F-15C pilots. Well, a lot of my squadron buddies at Holloman were former F-4 and F-5 pilots who were still fighting check and extend basic fighter manoeuvres, which involved flying a hard break into the bandit using the thrust and the turn rate ability of the F-15 [which] was enough to force the bandit to reposition. When the bandit repositioned, you took the G off the aeroplane to extend and get energy back, and when the bandit pitched back into you, you back on him. At the time, the F-15 community was just starting to employ rate fight concept versus check and extend. Using the rate fight, you maintained your energy and took advantage of the great turn rate of the F 15 and its radar's capability, invoking a two-circle fight versus a one-circle fight."

One-circle means the friendly aircraft turns towards the bandit using its tighter turn, smaller turn radius to get it in a favorable position before both aircraft have completed a half 180° turn. Two-circle means the friendly turns away from the bandit, because the friendly aircraft has a better turn rate, one that that will bring it into a favourable position after one full 360° turn.

US Air Force

Discussing the need to employ the rate fight, im said: "It was a big transition for me to go to ne rate fight, but Charly 'Bones' Shugg was a reat instructor for that, and proved to be good aining for me and improved how I employed ne aircraft, and how to better instruct students.

"Within a month or two of arriving at Tyndall, y squadron transitioned to the F-15C model. uring that time, I flew my F-15A from Tyndall to avis-Monthan Air Force Base for storage with ne Aerospace Maintenance And Regeneration roup. I taxied down the long, lonely taxiway out) the boneyard and shut it down with no write ps; it was a great aeroplane, that got chopped p. To me, the F-15C was a much-improved ersion, equipped with a better radar, chaff and are dispensers and more reliable engines.

"We [the 95th TFTS] made one deployment) Naval Air Station Miramar, California and ew against F-14 Tomcats, they were F-14A+ odels equipped with the original radar and ew engines. It was interesting to fight an -14A+ Tomcat that had a lot more thrust than ne original model.

"My last F-15 flight at Tyndall was a 2 v 2 cenario against F/A-18 Hornets. It was a strange feeling knowing that it was my last flight in an F-15, and my last flight in an air force aeroplane. When I walked out to the jet, I noticed that my aircraft had no weapon pylons or tanks fitted. That meant I had a lot less fuel than my wingman's jet and no infrared-guided missiles, just inert radar-guided missiles. We hadn't briefed for this scenario because it was unknown to us, but we continued because we wanted to turn and burn with the Hornets. The first engagement was briefed for no pre-merge kills which was challenging against two Hornets that could turn very tightly in the fight in which I had no infrared-guided missiles.

"I was the number two of two. We did a max power take-off which in my slick jet meant 660 knots by the departure end of the runway, got a double rate beeper on the G limiter in the pull up into the vertical, managed to lock-up the lead aircraft and still had 100 knots in the closure on him, while going straight up; performance wise, that was awesome. I left the air force in January 1993 and within a couple of weeks joined United Airlines for a 28-year commercial career."

Top-down view of an F-15A showing the pilot climbing the crew ladder. US Air Force

SUBSCRIBE TODAY!

UK Airshow previews RIAT and Farnborough
AIRFORCES MONTHLY
Fighting for the future
RAF Combat Air issues
Defence dilemmas
For new UK government
Korean Phantom farewell
Reflection and sentiment at Suwon
The unscripted conflict
New tactics in Ukraine War
Europe's future missile shield
Protection from Putin
Swiss road exercise
Bringing back the past
Receive A Free Gift

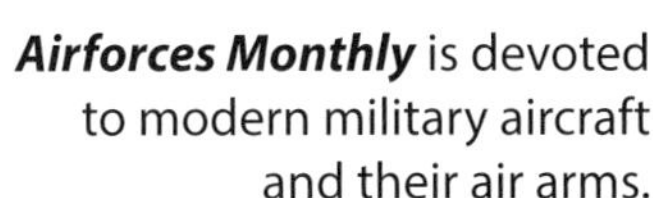

RAMSTEIN GUNSLINGERS NATO FIGHTERS IN 1V1 DOGFIGHTS
COMBAT AIRCRAFT JOURNAL
FIRST OF A THREE-PART SERIES
SALUTING 50 YEARS OF F-16s
PART ONE – CURRENT USAF OPERATORS
BLACKBIRDS OVER BRITAIN
50th anniversary of SR-71 in UK
HEATING UP ALASKA
In Red Flag 24-2
FRENCH C-135s
Then there were three
Receive A Free Gift

Airforces Monthly is devoted to modern military aircraft and their air arms.

Combat Aircraft Journal is renowned for being America's best-selling military aviation magazine.

om our online shop...

collections/subscriptions

**Free 2nd class P&P on all UK & BFPO orders. Overseas charges apply.*

F-106A 57-2470 assigned to the Massachusetts Air National Guard's 102nd Fighter Interceptor Wing shortly after the ejection of an AIR-2A Genie rocket from the aircraft's weapon bay. It took 0.23 seconds from ejection to forward flight. US Air National Guard

Delta Darts and Eagles

Reed Hamilton flew many types of fighter aircraft including the F-106 Delta Dart and the F-15 Eagle with the Massachusetts Air National Guard.

After flying the F-4 Phantom with the active-duty air force, Reed Hamilton joined the New York Air National Guard. He flew two types, the F-86H Sabre fighter and then the A-37B attack aircraft, both while assigned to the 174th Tactical Fighter Group based at Hancock Field in Syracuse. Reed then transferred to the Massachusetts Air National Guard, flew the F-100D Super Sabre with the 102nd Tactical Fighter Wing when the wing was under the control of Tactical Air Command, and the F-106 Delta Dart with the 102nd Air Defense Wing under the control of Air Defense Command.

Discussing his time with the F-106. Reed said: "I checked out in the F-106 at Tyndall Air Force Base, Florida in 1975 with the 2nd Fighter Intercept Training Squadron. The eight-week course taught you how to fly the F-106 and conduct the interception mission, it was an interceptor by design, and had no air-to-ground capability. The F-106 carried air-to-air missiles in a missile bay located along the centre of the fuselage underside with huge bay doors that opened outwards. They were pneumatically controlled and opened fast. Two racks of missiles came down automatically; the forward rack carried Hughes radar-guided AIM-4F missiles, and the rear rack carried two Hughes AIM-4G infrared-guided missiles."

F-106A 57-2494 assigned to the Massachusetts Air National Guard's 102nd Fighter Interceptor Wing shadows a Soviet Air Force Tu-95 Bear-D *bomber over the western Atlantic in 1982. US Air National Guard*

The AIM-4F and AIM-4G had a higher speed and ceiling, longer range, better seeker systems and more powerful warheads than their predecessors. The AIM-4F had an improved radar guidance system with greater accuracy and increased resistance to enemy jamming; the AIM-4G had a more effective infrared detector.

According to the website F-106deltadart.com: "The missile bay door system operated on 3,000psi air pressure to drive the doors open in 1.5 seconds and after the selected munitions were fired closed in 0.75 seconds. A main air flask was charged to 3,000 psi, and the weapon system actuators worked at 1,500 psi via a regulator. The cycle time on the missile bay doors, however, did vary dependent on the weapon type were being

"My god, I'd never experienced anything like it. We were off the ground in 11 seconds at 160 knots and when you pulled the stick straight back into your lap, the ADI tumbled but you were going vertical."

fired. The AIR-2A Genie was fastest because it was ejected from the bay and took 0.23 seconds from ejection to forward flight. Hughes AIM-4 Super Falcon missiles launched from the racks fired two at a time, either both AIM-4F or both AIM-4Gs.

"The AIR-2A Genie was an air-to-air rocket with a nuclear warhead designed for use against formations of enemy bombers. It was the world's first nuclear-armed air-to-air interceptor weapon and consequently was the most powerful ever deployed by the US Air Force. It had no guidance system and was powered by a solid-propellant rocket motor."

Speaking about the Genie, Reed said: "Nuclear armed weapons were stored in a nuclear storage area and available in times of war only. Everything was top secret. I was never loaded with a nuclear weapon unless it was on training exercise. It was an unguided missile, like a rocket. You fired it, it left the aircraft, dropped down on a cable, the cable ignited the engine, and it accelerated to Mach 3. It was supposed to be able to take out a fleet of bombers, that was the whole idea of it. Bombers in the old days used to fly in close formations, they don't anymore."

DELTA DARTS IN MASSACHUSETTS

Describing the F-106 aircraft, Reed said: "It was a fast, high-altitude interceptor that enabled us to own the skies above 40,000 feet. It had an enormous Pratt & Whitney J75 engine with afterburner and was capable of cruising at Mach 0.93. In fact, when we used to go on cross country trips, we would fly up to 41,000 feet, well above all other commercial traffic, nobody was up there, so the controllers would clear us direct, which was wonderful. We would cruise climb, because the controllers would clear us all the way to 50,000 feet, we didn't have any restrictions on us whatsoever.

"We kept the power set where it was at the most economical cruise. But Mach 0.93 would soon go to Mach 0.95, 0.97 and 0.99, very close to Mach 1.0 when the plane might get a little squirrelly on the autopilot, and might start doing small fishtails, but that was the maximum cruise speed unless you wanted to go supersonic for short distances. For example, one morning I flew the wing's flight surgeon in the backseat to Andrews Air Force Base, Maryland outside of Washington DC. I met back with him at base operations at two o'clock. I said to him, 'do you want to get back to Cape Cod quickly'? 'Sure', he said. I filed a flight plan with Washington Center for an unrestricted climb though I was doubtful it would be granted because it's congested airspace. Unbelievably, they cleared us for unrestricted climb, and we flew all the way back to Cape Cod from Andrews Air Base in 32 minutes. While over the water we flew at Mach 1.7 so that's an example of the aircraft's versatility.

"We could fly from Cape Cod to McChord Air Force Base in Washington State in two hops. The first hop was Cape Cod to Fargo, North Dakota where the aircraft was refuelled, and the second hop was from Fargo to McChord. Each hop was two-and-a-half hours, but we did not fly supersonic on those runs to conserve fuel.

F-106A 57-2467 assigned to the Massachusetts Air National Guard's 102nd Fighter Interceptor Wing with its braking chute deployed after landing at Otis Air National Guard Base. Note the Cape Cod legend on the side of the external fuel tanks. US Air National Guard

"My training course at Tyndall lasted about eight weeks. On return to Otis, I started to fly operational missions and sat alert during which the wing had lots of klaxon calls to scramble. The wing was famous in the early days for intercepts of Soviet Tu-95 *Bear* bombers. We received intelligence reports notifying us that Soviet bombers were airborne and to expect to see them in about six hours. Sure enough, they'd show up and we'd meet them near Greenland heading for a shoot box, an area of airspace from where the would orbit and simulate launching nuclear air-launched missiles at the United States. Air defence scramble missions had to have tanke support; they were given priority.

"The wing had responsibility to intercept any aircraft that broke the air defence identification zone or ADIZ which extended from the Canadian ADIZ around Nova Scotia down the east coast. Any aircraft penetrating the ADIZ without clearance would be

F-15A Eagle 77-0102 from the Massachusetts Air National Guard's 102nd Fighter Wing on a combat air patrol mission over New York City in support of Operation Noble Eagle in November 2001. US Air National Guard/Lieutenant Colonel Bill Ramsay

ntercepted. In support of that tasking, the 02nd Fighter Interceptor Wing maintained a etachment of four F-106s at Loring Air Force ase near the city of Limestone in the far north f Maine. It was home to the 42nd Bomb Wing quipped with B-52 bombers and KC-135 ankers, the four F-106s were held on alert."

Reed flew the F-106 with the 102nd Fighter nterceptor Wing, later the 102nd Fighter Ving between 1975 and 1987. In 1987, he vas named the squadron commander with esponsibility for the final disposition of the ving's 18 F-106 aircraft which were all flown to he boneyard at Davis-Monthan Air Force Base n Tucson, Arizona.

EAGLES IN MASSACHUSETTS

Discussing the lead-up to the 102nd Fighter nterceptor Wing re-equipping with the F-15 agle, Reed said: "In 1986, we had word that ve were to be given a new fighter plane, and was initially thought that we were going to be flying F-16s, but we really wanted the F-15 because it was an interceptor aircraft just like the F-106. Senator Ted Kennedy and Speaker of the House, Tip O'Neill were instrumental in bringing the F-15 to Otis.

"The F-15 transition proved to be the busiest five years of my entire US Air Force career. On a drill weekend in the summer of 1987, we invited Senator Kennedy to attend, and I appeared in a well-circulated photo shaking hands with the senator and handing him a huge silver key to the F-15 as a thanks to him for getting us the aeroplane.

"Starting in the spring of 1988, the 102nd was re-equipped with 20 F-15A and two F-15B aircraft transferred from the 5th Fighter Interceptor Squadron based at Minot Air Force Base, North Dakota, which was subsequently deactivated. The aircraft were about 10 years old, so I had responsibility for 22 F-15s worth $680 million which had to be accounted for and reported daily. I had to sign the papers every day which were sent to Headquarters Tactical Air Command at Langley Air Force Base, Virginia, it was quite a responsibility.

"We had a new manning document which gave me the authority to hire 12 additional pilots for two reasons. One, the F-15 aircraft required for the operating unit to have a greater number of pilots per aircraft than the F-106, and two, we increased the number of allocated aircraft from 18 F-106s to 22 F-15s.

"It was a busy time for me because I was interviewing and hiring pilots and maintaining my currency in the F-15 aircraft. As part of the transition, each pilot was given a preference sheet on which they listed their preferred F-15 training base and what time frame would work best in respect of their civilian career. There were two F-15 training bases, one was Luke Air Force Base near Phoenix, Arizona, and the other one was Tyndall Air Force Base near Panama City, Florida.

F-106A Delta Darts assigned to the Massachusetts Air National Guard's 102nd Fighter Interceptor Wing (nearest camera) parked on the flight line at Tyndall Air Force Base, Florida during a William Tell gunnery competition in 1984. US Air National Guard

"Not everybody got exactly what they wanted, but most people got close to what they wanted. In my case I opted for Tyndall where I started F-15 transition training in January 1988 with the same, but re-designated, squadron that I trained to fly the F-106 in 1974. Back then it was the 2nd Fighter Interceptor Training Squadron, in 1988 it was the 2nd Tactical Fighter Training Squadron, still using the same building!

"Our pilots were all very experienced and were given two options, the eight-week short course and the 12-week long course. No one could afford to be away from their civilian job for 12 weeks, so most went through the eight-week course."

F-15 TRAINING

The eight-week course started with two flights in an F-15B with an instructor pilot in the back seat. These were labelled TR1 and TR2, the first involved getting used to the feel of the aircraft and basic fighter manoeuvring. According to Reed, the F-15 flew like a dream and had tonnes more power than an F-106, especially down low.

Explaining, he said: "TR2 was called the gee whiz ride, the aircraft was in slick configuration, no tanks, so my instructor kept emphasising to not trap the landing gear, because it accelerated so fast. They wanted you to keep it low at 200 feet, gear up, flaps up, and at the end of the runway, to pull the stick straight back. My god, I'd never experienced anything like it. We were off the ground in 11 seconds at 160 knots

nd when you pulled the stick straight back nto your lap, the ADI tumbled but you were joing vertical. Just watching the airspeed, ve had 500 knots at the end of the runway, ncreasing to 510, 520, 530, 540, 550, 560, no kidding. The instructor said, look back behind you and it was like being at Cape Canaveral on a moon-shot. You were going straight up and accelerating. No fighter plane 'd flown before ever accelerated in a vertical climb. That convinced me I was in the right et. For TR3, you were in a jet on your own, your instructor was flying another F-15 on the wing.

"The F-15 was a complex aircraft and presented an entirely new world to any pilot new to it. The radar was totally different, the radar display was smack dab in front of you, in an F-106 it was down by your left knee. In an F-15, you did everything through the heads-up display or HUD, which was positioned straight ahead, in the centre of the windscreen, above the instrument panel. The HUD was your buddy, pretty much all flight information was displayed on it, which kept your eyes from looking down into the cockpit to read the gauges, because that could disorient you. The F-15 was designed such that the pilot would never have to look down into the cockpit. For example, there were 11 switches on the two throttles, one switch had five functions, depending on whether you moved it, up, down, left, right or pushed it. Using the switches was just like playing a piccolo, because you had to be very adept with your fingers. Anybody with any kind of hand issues would not have been able to fly the aeroplane.

> **"Senator Ted Kennedy and Speaker of the House, Tip O'Neill were instrumental in bringing the F-15 to Otis."**

"As part of the F-15 transition, I screened our pilots for F-15 training, but unfortunately, I didn't select four pilots because of various issues. This of course frustrated them, but in such a situation, it's what the commander must do. In general, our pilots were already good sticks, they already knew what the hell they were doing, especially in the air-to-air role for which they were specialists. They knew about radars, intercepts, how to find targets, how to lock them up and shoot them, which was what the F-15 training was all about. I don't think we had anybody wash out. We also hired new pilots, most were F-15 instructor pilots, one was a US Navy F-4 Phantom pilot, so by the end of 1988, once our pilots' transition training was complete, we had 42 highly qualified pilots."

HOLDING ALERT

Training was one thing, but as each pilot returned to Otis, they had to complete follow-on training, a series of missions to become mission capable (MC) and then mission ready (MR). Explaining, Reed said: "We wanted all but a few pilots to be MR, the higher-ranking officers usually qualified as MC. They were very good at flying the aeroplane, but they didn't have time to fly all the time because they were kept busy performing other duties. As one of those officers, in my 40s, I felt I had to fly six to eight missions a month to keep my hand in there. Some pilots flew more than that, and others flew less than that.

"Given the importance of holding alert, the squadron sat alert well before we had our ORI or operational readiness inspection. Officers from headquarters, Tactical Air Command Headquarters would visit the wing to assist us and unofficially evaluate us. During 1988, the four-aircraft detachment at Loring was manned with the experienced F-15 instructor pilots in the unit by that time."

Reed recalled times when he travelled to Loring on a Monday so he could sit a 24-hour alert and get some paperwork done during the oodles of quiet hours and travel back to Otis the following day.

Discussing the Loring alert, Reed said: "Most of the pilots that went to the detachment at Loring were standing alert for at least 48 hours and maybe more, they had plenty of time to rest and sleep. We had a detachment commander and an assistant commander permanently stationed at Loring to run the operation there.

"On one occasion when I was standing alert, the bell rang at 0345, so we were awakened, and quickly got into our gear. This was in February yet my young accomplice, a major, says 'we're not wearing poopy suits, are we'? I said, 'yeah, we are'. Regulations are what they are, we're wearing them because we're out over the ocean. Putting on the poopy suit involved this anti exposure suit that came down over your head and you had a zipper from your left wrist to your right wrist, and it was arduous to get into, cumbersome and

"In an F-15, you did everything through the heads-up display or HUD, which was positioned straight ahead, in the centre of the windscreen, above the instrument panel."

F-15A Eagle 76-0058 assigned to Massachusetts Air National Guard's 102nd Fighter Wing flies over Cape Cod, Massachusetts. Note the stylised Cape Code legend and harpoon motif on the side of the external fuel tank. US Air National Guard

wkward. Then you put your flight suit on ver your poopy suit, it meant a seven-minute cramble versus five minutes. The poopy uit was supposed to give you an extra hour f protection in the cold water to ward off ypothermia. I made the major wear the poopy uit even though he said he didn't want to, but hat's too bad.

"We scrambled in the middle of a very cold, tarry, clear sky, night and were vectored outh towards the coast, which was puzzling, ecause we were usually vectored east but

F-15A Eagle 76-0021 assigned to Massachusetts Air National Guard's 102nd Fighter Wing flies over the city of Boston, Massachusetts. US Air National Guard

we followed the instructions as given by the controllers. Somewhere east of Bangor, Maine at about 35,000 feet, we finally got a radar contact. It turned out to be a high-tailed twin engine turboprop aeroplane, lights out, heading northwest toward Montreal. We were instructed to trail it, but they didn't ask us to get its registration number. Well, my wingman, who was a young major said he was going to get the numbers. I told him to be careful. We always had one aircraft positioned three miles back from the other aircraft, which was on the target. This was done just in case the target got frisky and did something stupid and the pilot flying the aircraft in trail could shoot him down in a heartbeat.

"Somehow, thanks perhaps to the moonlight, my wingman got the aircraft's registration number which he radioed into headquarters. By this point we were heading to Canadian airspace, which meant getting clearance from the Canadian authorities to enter their airspace. Which we did. The rogue aircraft was heading for an uninhabited area to the northwest of Montreal. We carefully watched the rogue aircraft to observe if any drugs were jettisoned and could tell the aircraft was loaded down with drugs. The

F-15A Eagle 77-0100 from the Massachusetts Air National Guard's 102nd Fighter Wing on a combat air patrol mission over Long Island in support of Operation Noble Eagle in November 2001. The aircraft's tail has stylised markings for the 101st Fighter Squadron based at Otis Air National Guard Base. US Air National Guard/Lieutenant Colonel Bill Ramsay

F-15A Eagles 77-0111 and 77-0113 assigned to Massachusetts Air National Guard's 102nd Fighter Wing fly over Cape Cod, Massachusetts. Both aircraft are painted in a low-visibility two-tone colour scheme. US Air National Guard

Canadians requested we leave before the rogue aircraft got to its destination, besides which our fuel load was nearing bingo RTB, and we were denied a tanker, so we were low on fuel when we landed at Loring. It's likely that the rogue aircraft had taken off from Panama, but whatever its departure location it was the first drug intercept that our squadron made.

"After the fall of the Berlin Wall in November 1989, no Russian bombers were flying across the North Atlantic, so our intercepts were more of a mundane variety, like an airliner off course, for which we had to report its heading, speed, direction, and airline. We didn't normally get anywhere near an airliner because it would scare the passengers, so we stayed below and behind the aircraft, but of course we weren't going to shoot down an airliner."

WILLIAM TELL AND RED FLAG

In the days of the F-106, the 102nd Fighter Interceptor Wing participated in William Tell, a biennial aerial gunnery competition held at Tyndall Air Force Base, Florida. Each team competed in live-fire exercises against towed banner targets using the aircraft's cannon, and against full-scale aerial targets for air-to-air missile engagements.

"I felt I had to fly six to eight missions a month to keep my hand in there. Some pilots flew more than that."

When the 102nd flew the F-15 it participated in a lot of exercises including Exercise Red Flag at Nellis Air Force Base, Nevada. Discussing Red Flag, Reed said: "They were interesting evolutions because each aircraft was loaded with an air combat manoeuvring instrumentation or ACMI pod which recorded every single manoeuvre

that your aeroplane made and those of the simulated adversary aircraft. This made it easy to discern who shot who and when, how, and what missile was used. We took turns flying for either the friendly Blue or opposing Red Air force.

"In those days, we were trying to take beyond visual range missile shots at ranges over 10 miles and then use the gun if you merged with the opposing aircraft, turning, and burning in a dogfight. One thing we did at the merge in the F-15 was pull the power back, because you didn't want a huge heat signature out your back end inside 10 miles, because the opposing fighter could lock on and get an infrared-guided missile on you. We'd always flew to the merge at 500 knots, and at 10 miles, we'd go to half power and slow down, maybe to 460 knots by the merge, which was our turning speed, which was perfect.

> **"We carried four AIM-7 Sparrow and four AIM-9 Sidewinder air-to-air missiles, which were nasty, you could shoot yourself down if you didn't know what you were doing."**

"We also deployed to Tyndall for the Weapon System Evaluation Program [WSEP] to shoot missiles and fire the M61A1 six-barrel gatling gun. It fires 100 rounds per second and holds 942 rounds in an enclosed circular drum housed in the forward right part of the aeroplane: no ammunition was expended off board the aircraft. If you tried to fire a small burst, it was impossible to fire less than 100 rounds. During WSEP we were tasked to kill eight aeroplanes with eight missiles, and three more aeroplanes with the gun. We carried four AIM-7 Sparrow [replaced by AIM-120 AMRAAM] and four AIM-9 Sidewinder air-to-air missiles, which were nasty, you could shoot yourself down if you didn't know what you were doing, because it's a launch and leave missile."

NOTHING LIKE EXPERIENCE

It's no secret that Air National Guard units are manned with lots of experienced personnel who acquit themselves better because of their level of experience in flying and maintaining aircraft as Reed explained: "We had guys that had been flying the aeroplane for years. Remember, active-duty units rotated their personnel so fast that nobody stayed in the unit for more than three years, so we felt the guard pilots were a little bit better, and we always felt we kicked some ass. Similarly, the experience of the maintainers assigned to an Air National Guard wing was head and shoulders above active duty.

"When serving with the New York Air National Guard at Syracuse equipped with the F-86 Sabre, prior to one mission sat in an aircraft I gave the start signal. My sergeant climbed to the top rung of the crew access ladder, which is very unusual, looked over my shoulder, and I looked at him and said, 'hey, sarge, you're clear to go stand by the fire bottle'. 'No', he says, 'I don't want you to screw up'. I looked at his sleeve, and he was an E-7, a seniomaster sergeant, well if that had been with the active duty the person attending to my jet might have been an E-3, airman, or an E-4, a senior airman, but it was not uncommon, most of the time I had master sergeants working on my jet. At Otis, our maintenance people were really experienced.

"As commander of a fighter squadron with 42 pilots and numerous enlisted folks, I had a lot of other responsibilities and didn't get all the plum missions due to other commitments. I felt like I had used up most of my nine lives, and that it was the right time to leave the guard, why not go out while you're on top? So, I retired in 1991 after 28 years of service, one of the few people that was qualified as combat ready in the F-86 Sabre [in 1969] and the F-15 Eagle [in 1989], just the luck of the draw being in the guard."

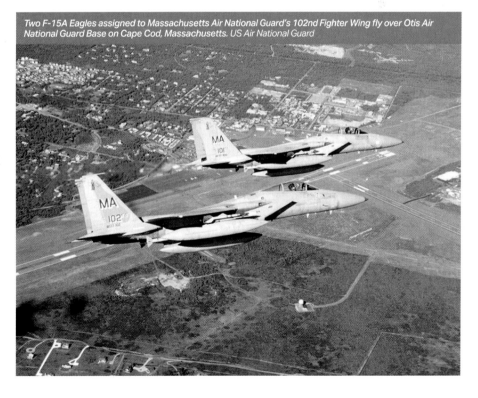

Two F-15A Eagles assigned to Massachusetts Air National Guard's 102nd Fighter Wing fly over Otis Air National Guard Base on Cape Cod, Massachusetts. US Air National Guard

Eagle Driver to Lieutenant General

Andy Croft served as an F-15C pilot with a variety of units, not least the US Air Force Weapons School. After a remarkable career, he retired as a lieutenant general.

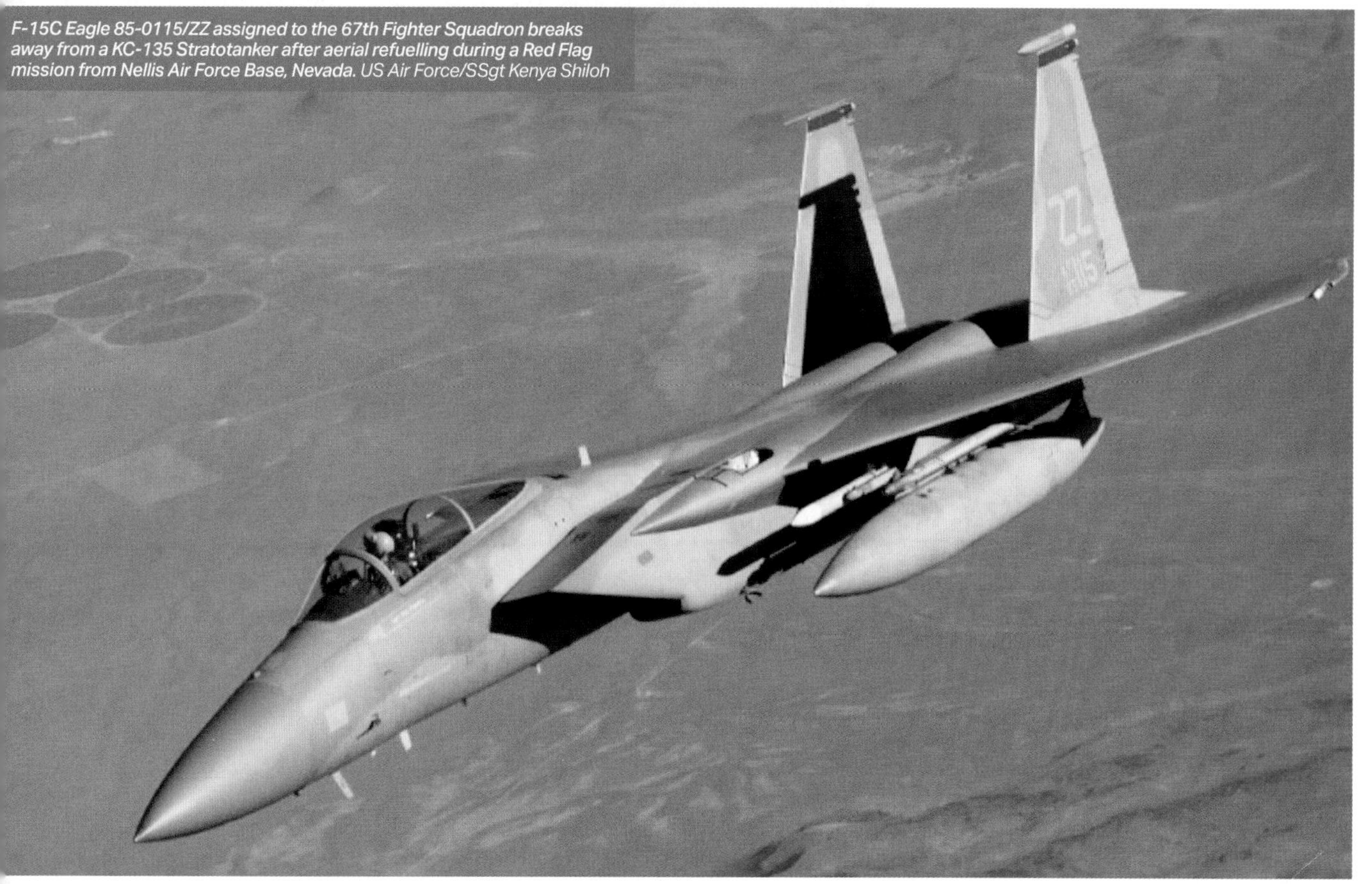

F-15C Eagle 85-0115/ZZ assigned to the 67th Fighter Squadron breaks away from a KC-135 Stratotanker after aerial refuelling during a Red Flag mission from Nellis Air Force Base, Nevada. *US Air Force/SSgt Kenya Shiloh*

Crew chiefs assigned to the 67th Fighter Squadron stand ready to assist an F-15 Eagle as the pilot taxies to parking at Komatsu Air Base, Japan. The squadron participated in the bilateral aviation training relocation program with the Japanese Air Self Defense Force. *US Air Force/SSgt Amber Jacobs*

Andy Croft completed pilot training with the 14th Flying Training Wing at Columbus Air Force Base, Mississippi in May 1990. He was selected for the F-15 Eagle which required him to complete Lead in Fighter Training (LIFT) at Holloman Air Force Base, New Mexico flying the AT-38B with the 479th Tactical Training Wing.

Describing the LIFT course, Andy said: "The three-month course trained students in the culture of being a fighter pilot, more so than the actual manoeuvring of the aeroplane."

He successfully completed LIFT in September 1990 and was assigned to the 325th Tactical Fighter Wing based at Tyndall Air Force Base, Florida to take the F-15 B-course with the 95th Tactical Fighter Training Squadron.

> **"When I looked down at the oil gauge, the system was losing pressure. It was clear I was losing a lot of oil out of one of the engines."**

Discussing his first impression of the F-15, Andy said: "It was huge compared to anything else I'd ever flown, the T-37B Tweet and the T-38A Talon. The T-38 was very responsive and very lightweight compared to the F-15 which seemed like a monster when I first started flying it. On my second solo ride [flight] while flying over the Gulf of Mexico, I heard a strange rhythmic vibration coming from the back of the aeroplane, which to me, even though I only had about 10 hours in it total, did not sound right. When I looked down at the oil gauge, the system was losing pressure. It was clear I was losing a lot of oil out of one of the engines. The dash one checklist, which is the tech manual, states you should never operate the engine with zero oil pressure, and when the pressure is less than 15, you should consider shutting the engine down. So, I did. I radioed my instructor, who was the flight lead. I said, I've just shut down the right engine because I'm losing oil pressure. I declared an inflight emergency. Because the aeroplane has quite a bit of thrust, it was not difficult to fly with just one engine and my aircraft was flying well so we returned to Tyndall, flew a straight in approach, and landed. The squadron gave me a safety award for saving the engine, running it for any length of time with no oil would have seized and destroyed the engine.

"At the time we had about two or three fighter weapons school graduates in our squadron serving as instructor pilots. They were noticeably better than any of the other pilots, but by quite a large margin. They had attended the F-15 weapons school, served on an operational squadron, and then went to Tyndall to instruct. With as much as seven years of experience in the F-15 it was amazing to witness how much better they were than everybody else in terms of skill and ability when briefing a mission, flying the aircraft, and debriefing."

Andy graduated from the B-course in February 1991 and was then assigned to the 27th Fighter Squadron, a component unit of the 1st Fighter Wing at Langley Air Force Base, Virginia. In August 1990, he knew his first operational assignment would be with the 27th Tactical Fighter Squadron based at Langley Air Force Base, Virginia, the second F-15 squadron deployed to Saudi Arabia for Operation Desert Shield before Desert Storm. Talking through his course of events, Andy said: "I missed Operations Desert Shield and Desert Storm by about eight months because I joined the 27th Tactical Fighter Squadron in March 1991 after the squadron had returned from Saudi Arabia. I was the first lieutenant to join the squadron after it had completed a nine-month combat tour. I served with the 27th for four years [1991-1995], qualified as an instructor pilot and mission commander, and during that time, deployed to Saudi Arabia twice in support of Operation Southern Watch and flew fly zone enforcement missions over southern Iraq.

"At the end of my tour at Langley, in 1995 I was assigned back to Tyndall Air Force Base as an instructor [academic and pilot] with the 2nd Fighter Squadron. During that tour, in June 1997, I attended the US Air Force Fighter Weapons School at Nellis, returned to Tyndall for another eight months, and then in early

Airmen check over F-15C 80-0002/WA on the end-of-runway ramp at Nellis Air Force Base, Nevada prior to a mission in support of the US Air Force Weapons School. Paul Ridgway

998 started my new assignment with the 8th Fighter Wing based at Kadena Air Base in kinawa as the weapons officer with the 67th ighter Squadron for nearly two years and ıen as the 18th Fighter Wing weapons officer or my last eight months. The wing weapons fficer oversaw all weapons officers assigned the three resident fighter squadrons, wrote e flying standards documents, standardised ictics, and flew with all three squadrons.

"It was a busy squadron which conducted aining deployments to mainland Japan, the epublic of Korea, Singapore, and Thailand. In ıe summer of 1999, the squadron deployed Incirlik Air Base, Turkey in support of peration Northern Watch and flew fly zone nforcement missions over northern Iraq.

"Our route was from Okinawa to Alaska, hich is about seven or eight hours of flying, ıen from Alaska all the way to Lajes on the zores, which is a heck of a long flight. We flew ith a KC-10 most of the way across Canada, outing just south of Hudson Bay. When we got the Newfoundland coast near St John's we had enough fuel in the jets that we didn't need the tanker for the crossing of the Atlantic to, so the tanker went home before we had crossed the Canadian coastline, leaving the Eagles to fly all the way across the Atlantic to the Azores without the tanker. The F-15 was built to fly long range when fitted with three external tanks.

"Upon arrival in the Azores, the weather at Lajes was terrible, so we all had to fly PAR approaches. In addition, eight F-16s happened to arrive at the same time meaning that 14 fighter aircraft needed individual approaches given the weather conditions. Because my aircraft had the most fuel in the tanks, I was the last to land. By the time I had to get out of the cockpit, I had been sitting in the ejection seat for 15 hours, which is a long time, and it was hard to stand up and get out of the aeroplane after that amount of time. From the Azores we flew to Incirlik."

MONKEY SEE, MONKEY DO

Andy was one of six students in his F-15C class at the weapons school between January and June 1997. Discussing his experiences

> **"Our route was from Okinawa to Alaska, which is about seven or eight hours of flying, then from Alaska all the way to Lajes on the Azores, which is a heck of a long flight."**

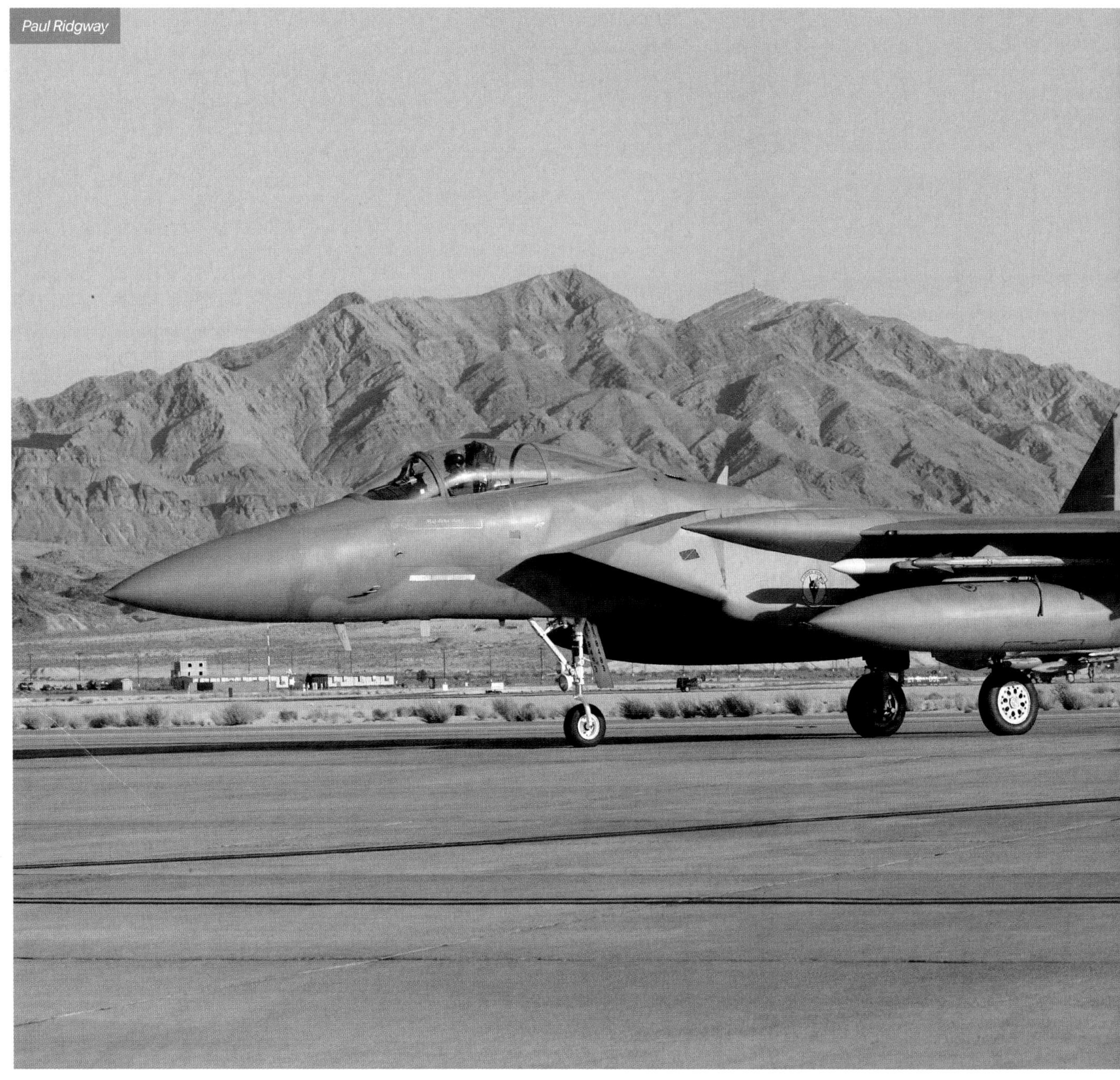
Paul Ridgway

there, he said: "It was an extremely intense and difficult course. The A-10, F-15C, F-15E, and F-16 were the primary fighters at the time. Each student was hand selected from a pecking order at your fighter wing. Once you started the application process, instructors from the weapons school came to your squadron to fly with prospective students. It was akin to an initial assessment: can the student make it through the school?

"The course comprised a series of extremely difficult sorties, about 42 from my recollection. The first 12 were 1 v 1, then 2 v 1, then 2 v 4 engagements, gradually larger scenarios, until the end of the course when you fought as part of a very large force with as many as 50 aeroplanes.

"The concept of weapons school training was known as see-do. You saw the ride first, the instructor briefs, flies and debriefs the mission, when you were number two, flying as the wingman. So, you observed the ride as a pilot, but you were not leading the ride. Then you flew a second ride as the flight lead, so you were leading it. We referred to the concept as 'monkey see, monkey do'. The bottom line, the mission was demonstrated to you, and then you had to repeat it as the leader of the of the mission. It was difficult. Around 25 to 30% of the sorties that you flew, you failed and had to be flown again, but the elimination rate was small; for every 15 students that went through the course, maybe one was eliminated, because the filtering process before students arrived was very effective.

> **"By the time I had to get out of the cockpit, I had been sitting in the ejection seat for 15 hours."**

"The missions were extremely complicate difficult, high pressure. Unique to the F-15 in those days was the debrief, it lasted for hour It was not uncommon to fly a one-and-a-half-hour mission, and then debrief for eight or nine hours. For one mission we briefed at 0900 in the morning and finished the debrief at 0600 the next morning, so a 21-hour even from start to finish. Many of the other fighter divisions were incredulous that we would debrief the missions for so long. But that's where all the learning was, the debrief of an F-15 mission was primarily a review of the radar tape. We watched the radar operation from start to finish, minute by minute. We would not skip over any of it. In fact, much of it was done in slow motion to see if you as the pilot, saw everything the radar saw or not. That was really the key, because the pilots flying the aeroplane were very good at disciplined radar work with the ability to do things at long range, meaning over 30 miles. You're doing intercept geometry and manoeuvring to put yourself in a position of advantage from very long range.

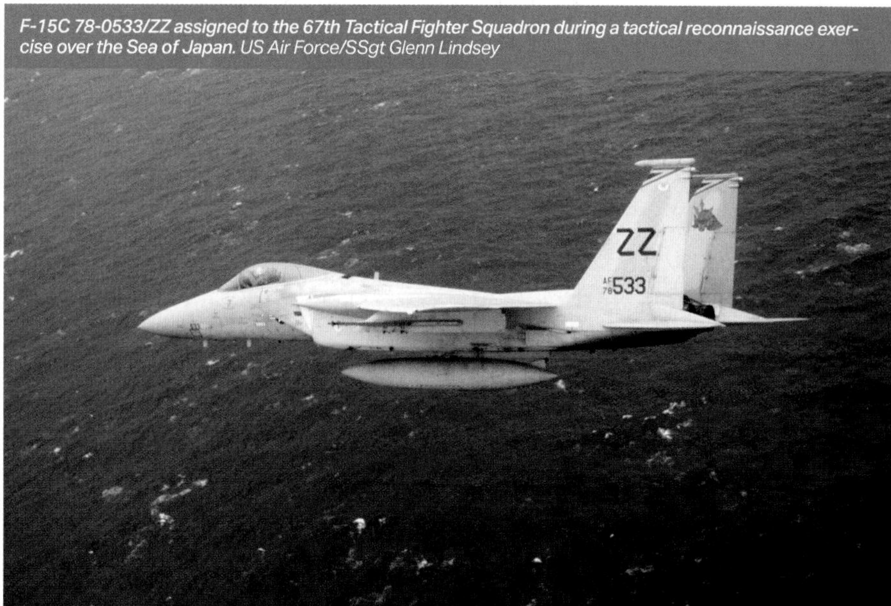

F-15C 78-0533/ZZ assigned to the 67th Tactical Fighter Squadron during a tactical reconnaissance exercise over the Sea of Japan. US Air Force/SSgt Glenn Lindsey

"Briefing and debriefing were probably the ey aspects of weapons school: 70-minute rief, 60-90-minute sortie and anywhere from our to 12 hours of debrief, depending on the omplexity of the sortie."

Discussing the robustness of the threat resentation provided by the aggressor to ne F-15 weapons school, Andy said: "The ggressors were extremely professional in hat they did, and they did their best to try nd simulate Soviet bloc tactics, particularly a Red Flag scenario. The weapons school sed them a little bit differently. We gave nem specific parameters on what kind of roblem we wanted them to present to us, esigned to challenge the students in various cenarios. So, we would either ask them to onduct certain types of electronic jamming r electronic attack, we would ask them to fly pecific formations to make it difficult, but not npossible, to sort out what was happening. Ve gave them a general idea of when we anted them to manoeuvre so we could meet ne objectives of the mission we were flying, nd they were very good at that. The other thing unique to their style of flying was their ground control intercept or GCI controllers who were very prescriptive, so turn this way, turn that way, like the Russians would do it, and they had great control. So, they were very good at presenting the exact presentation that we asked for. If there was an error made on the F-15 side, they would punish the mistakes by 'shooting down' one of the F-15s either within visual range or beyond visual range.

"The other unique thing was that we always did permanent kill removal, meaning that if you got shot down two minutes into a 30-minute mission, you went home. There was no regeneration. In many training environments, you stopped and then started again. It was great motivation to not get shot because you had to go home early.

"The aggressors were very good at presenting tactical problems for us, especially in intercept geometry, based on the sort of script we gave them. When the aggressors flew in Red Flag, it was a different and changing problem set - they started off with relatively simple problem sets, and gradually increased the complexity through the two weeks of flying. By the second week, you'd see their highest level of tactical problem presentation.

"At weapons school we flew against other F-15 squadrons from around the country. Those squadrons deployed to Nellis to support the weapons school students by providing different presentations and problem sets as Red Air. This loosened up the aggressor squadron workload and provided different Red Air opponents for us. The aggressor squadron's primary task was to support Exercises Red Flag and Green Flag, the operational test squadron based at Nellis, and to support other units at their home station: not specifically to support the weapons school.

"When I left the weapons school in June 1997 I couldn't to wait to get out of the place and remember looking in my rearview mirror driving away from the Las Vegas Strip, thinking, I'm never coming back. It was such a gruelling experience. One thing I noticed as a student, when I went into work in the morning, the instructors were there, and when I left in the evening, at whatever time, they were still there. I thought, my gosh, I'm here most of my day and these guys are here before me and after me, so it was a grind."

All US Air Force Weapons School aircraft are assigned to a squadron, such as the 433rd Weapons Squadron flying F-15C Eagles. All aircraft are assigned to the 57th Wing based at Nellis. F-15C 83-0019/WA seen with tail markings for the 57th Wing, landing on runway 21R at Nellis. Paul Ridgway

Discussing how his weapons school course and graduation changed him and its application to becoming an instructor pilot, Andy said: "There's often a desire to try and recreate weapons school in your own squadron, which is a little bit onerous for everybody else, especially the students because they can't absorb too much information. If you debriefed for longer than two hours, you started to lose the attention span. One of the challenges for a weapons school graduate was transitioning from a very tense learning environment back to the environment of a regular fighter squadron. You had to dial back and reduce your expectations, because at that point you were so used to working at such a high level following the six-month course. It was akin to learning the highest-level calculus then going back to teach basic arithmetic and realising the students are not ready for calculus.

"A lot of the weapon officer's job in the squadron is to find the next people to go to weapons school. I flew with other instructor pilots who were thinking of applying to figure out who were on pace as the number one, two, and three candidates for the school's next application round. Since the school ran a class every six months, you went through the process often. Much of it was assessing who should not attend weapons school. When I returned from the weapons school to Tyndall as an instructor, I trained a lot of young students that I eventually served with in subsequent fighter squadron assignment, which was enjoyable.

"Weapons school enabled you to go much farther in your air force career because it demonstrated you were tactically capable. As an example, from my class of six, two of us retired as three-star generals, one retired as a two-star general, and the other three all made it to colonel. Once you graduated from weapons school, you could go much farther in the air forc because you were recognised as an expert."

NELLIS BECKONS AGAIN

"During the summer of 2001, after serving as the advanced programs manager with the Air Warfare Center, I was asked to go back to the weapons school to serve as an instructor

"I remember looking in my rearview mirror driving away from the Las Vegas Strip, thinking, I'm never coming back."

During the final years of the weapons school F-15C division's existence, it was designated the 433rd Weapons Squadron. F-15C Eagle 83-0041/WA with tail markings for the squadron commander takes off from Nellis on a curriculum sortie. Paul Ridgway

and operations officer for the F-15C division of the US Air Force Weapons School. When you returned as an instructor, you had to go through an entire upgrade process. You had to fly all the missions again before you were qualified as an instructor, and it was a gruelling process. The instructor upgrade programme was an abridged version of the full weapons school course. For example, a student flew 12 basic fighter manoeuvring sorties, four offensive, four defensive, and four nose-to-nose, when you returned as an instructor, you flew one of each. Even though you'd been flying operationally, when you returned to the weapons school, you soon realised that the instructors were a much higher calibre, and it took a while to even match them, so it was a bit humbling. Generally, the school only invited back the top two from a class of six students."

During his time serving as a weapons school instructor, one of the most notable events was 9/11. On the day, the F-15C division was deployed at Tyndall Air Force Base in Florida for a live weapons shoot. Explaining the events, Andy said: "Each student flew three missions, one to fire the gun at a towed target and two to fire a live missile. On that fateful day we were scheduled to fire the gun. We had finished the briefing and stood at the operations desk waiting to get the tail numbers of our jets. A TV screen showed smoke bellowing from the World Trade Centre in New York, but we didn't know what had happened because we'd been in the brief. One of the people behind the desk said an aeroplane had hit the building but didn't know how big the aeroplane was. As we watched, the second aeroplane hit the second tower. I'll never forget, our vice wing commander who was stood with us said 'threatcon delta' which means the worst threat condition, clearly, we were under attack. Within a minute, the entire base went to threatcon delta. We were in complete lockdown; we couldn't leave the building, and nobody was allowed on or off base.

"I could see our crew chiefs, mechanics, and ammo troops on the flight line from where I was standing. As the operations officer, the number two officer on the squadron, I used a radio to call Mark, our senior master sergeant running the show on the flight line.

I said, 'Mark, load all the jets with three tanks and any live missiles you can get'. The jets were already loaded with 20mm rounds ready for the gun shooting mission scheduled that day. The flight line became a scene of much activity. Within a couple hours, our crew chiefs, mechanics, and ammo troops had loaded external fuel tanks and live missiles on the jets. It was amazing how quickly they reacted, remember we were not a combat unit, we were a training unit, but we were ready to respond.

"As it turned out, we never got called because the resident 325th Fighter Wing at Tyndall did all the flying. And I'll never forget that night, it was raining, and it seemed like every five or 10 minutes, another F-15 four-ship would take off on afterburner heading to fly CAPs over major cities all over the country. That was a Tuesday, by Thursday we were cleared to fly back to Nellis, so eight Eagles and four Strike Eagles took off together. There was not a single aeroplane airborne in United States airspace, except for fighters over cities. When we called Jacksonville Center, the air traffic controller cleared us direct to Las Vegas because there was nobody else in our way. We flew across the country, aerial refuelled with a tanker halfway across, and I remember there were no blips on my radar scope out to a range over 150 miles, and not a single person talking. It was eerie, flying across the United States without another aeroplane airborne.

"As we watched, the second aeroplane hit the second tower. I'll never forget, our vice wing commander who was stood with us said 'threatcon delta'."

Lieutenant Andrew 'Sparky' Croft. US Air Force

Since there was nobody else out there, we flew 12 line abreast, probably 15 miles across, all contrailing. Air traffic control agencies across the United States received calls from people who saw us contrailing, because you didn't normally see something like that.

"My instructor tour with the weapons school was an extremely satisfying assignment, though I'd never worked so hard in my life, combat was less stressful and less time consuming than weapons school. Once I'd completed that tour, frankly, I felt like I could do almost anything. The other challenge was trying to balance family life with my work, there was not a lot of dinner time with my children during those three years because the schedule was so variable and so extreme, but we all got through it."

After his time as a weapons school instructor came to an end, in 2003, Andy went to Air Command and Staff College at Maxwell Air Force Base, Alabama.

After that, Andy had to get back into the command sequence, so in August 2004 he was assigned to Eglin Air Force Base, Florida to serve as the chief of the base command post and as an instructor pilot with the 58th Fighter Squadron. He was due to be the operations officer for a year or two and then become a squadron commander. However, the plan was interrupted because the commander of the F-15C 433rd Weapons Squadron was selected to command the Thunderbirds aerial demonstration team. This meant there was nobody qualified to be the commander of the 433rd, so in May 2005 they asked Andy, he took command a couple of weeks later.

Explaining the challenges of this new tour with the weapons school, Andy said: "Given the requirements placed on me as the squadron commander to attend meetings and run the squadron, it was difficult to stay proficient with the curriculum and not become the limitation to an entire formation. If you skipped a certain phase of the course, you were not as well prepared for the next phase. The course followed a building block approach. It was difficult to be a good commander and simultaneously remain proficient enough to fly in some of the most difficult missions.

"The most significant thing that happened during my time as the 433rd commander was the impending planned replacement of the F-15 with the F-22. Under the original F-22 procurement the plan was to stand up an F-22 weapons school squadron. But it became obvious that the F-22 community was not going to be large enough to support an individual squadron by itself. So, we combined the F-22 with the F-15 in the 433rd for economy of scale because we needed people doing scheduling, running the range, and for kill assessment. There was insufficient manpower available to run two independent squadrons. Consequently, F-15s and F-22s were operated by the one squadron, sometimes they were flown together, sometimes separately.

"We also started placing some weapons officers into the F-22 so some of the graduates finished the F-15 weapons school and became the weapons officer for an F-22 squadron, even though they had not completed a weapons school course in the F-22. We had to do it because we needed that level of expertise in the new aeroplane. So, for about five years, the F-15 weapons school supported the graduates for both the F-22 and the F-15. That was key to try and achieve the right manpower mix for two aeroplanes to ensure the F-22 had the same standard and quality of pilots as the F-15. My command tour with the 433rd Weapons Squadron was my last assignment in the F-15."

COLLEGES AND COMMANDS

"After attending Naval War College in Newport, Rhode Island, I was assigned to

F-15D 83-0050/WA turns onto the final approach of runway 21R at Nellis Air Force Base. Paul Ridgway

Lieutenant Andrew Croft (fourth from left) poses with his B-course classmates in front of an F-15 Eagle at Tyndall air Force Base, Florida in May 1990. Andy Croft

NATO as the executive officer, Allied Air omponent Command Headquarters, Izmir, ırkey, then served as a strategic planner ır the Joint Staff in Arlington, Virginia, then s the 12th Operations Group Commander t Randolph Air Force Base, Texas where I ew the T-6A Texan as an instructor with ıe 559th Flying Training Squadron. In June 012 I was selected to be the commander, 9th Wing at Holloman Air Force Base, New lexico. At the time, the 49th was equipped ith F-22s and MQ-9 Reapers. I checked ıt in the F-22 but didn't get very many ours in it.

"I went to Peterson Air Force Base in Colorado Springs for a year to serve as the vice director of operations with headquarters North American Aerospace Defense Command. After gaining promotion to brigadier general and I went back to Randolph to serve as Air Education and Training Command's director for plans, programmes, requirements, and assessments when the main programme was acquisition of the T-X. I worked on the requirements for the aeroplane when the competitors were Lockheed Martin, Boeing, Northrop Grumman, and Leonardo. That was a two-year tour, then in April 2017 I went to Baghdad as the senior US Air Force officer with target engagement authority for Operation Inherent Resolve in the fight against ISIS [the so-called Islamic State]. In August 2018, I went to Davis-Monthan Air Force Base, Arizona and served as the 12th Air Force commander where I flew the A-10 and clocked up 150 hours. It's an outstanding aircraft. In that job I was also the air component commander for US Southern Command and then became the deputy commander for two years before I retired in 2023. I was sad to go but it was a great career including 2,800 hours on the F-15."

"It was eerie, flying across the United States without another aeroplane airborne. Since there was nobody else out there, we flew 12 line abreast, probably 15 miles across, all contrailing."

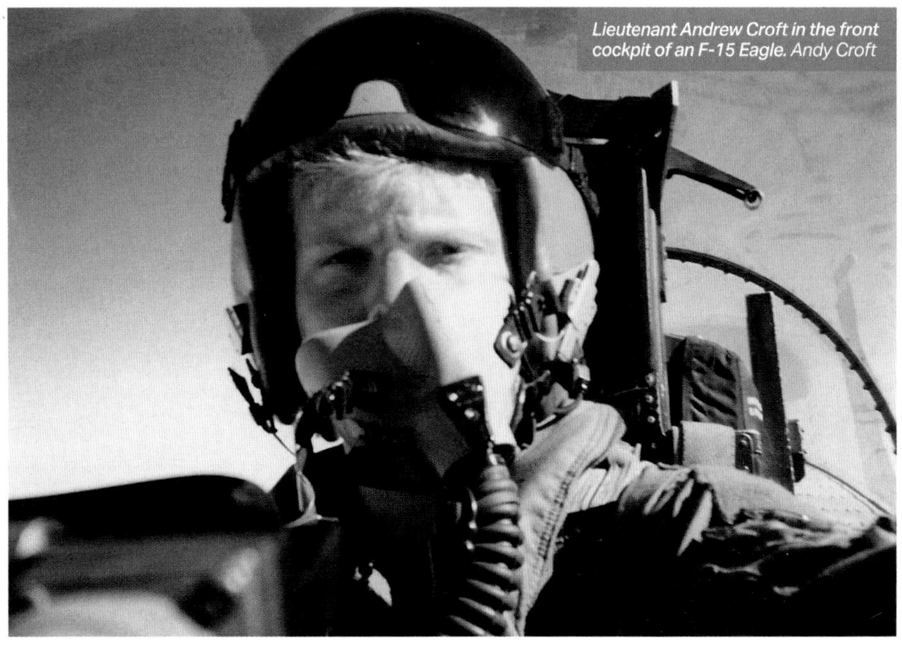

Lieutenant Andrew Croft in the front cockpit of an F-15 Eagle. Andy Croft

At the Heart of a Strike

When Neil Allen joined the US Air Force, he wanted to fly the F-4 Phantom, but a policy change meant he was selected for navigator training.

Later in his career, Neil Allen served as the commander of the 479th Flying Training Group based Naval Air Station Pensacola, Florida. US Air Force

T-43A 72-0288/RA assigned to the 12th Flying Training Wing based at Randolph Air Force Base, Texas was originally assigned to the 323rd Flying Training Wing based at Mather Air Force Base, California where Neil Allen trained on the type. US Air Force

At the time Neil Allen joined the USAF, navigator training was conducted by the 323rd Flying Training Wing based at Mather Air Force Base in California. The specialised undergraduate programme was conducted using the T-37B Tweet and the T-43A, a modified Boeing 737-200. After a brief phase of common training, navigator students were selected for one of three specialised tracks: fighter/attack/reconnaissance; tanker/transport/bomber; and electronic warfare.

Neil was selected for the fighter/attack/reconnaissance (FAR) track and initially completed four flights in the T-37B to learn basic airmanship, low-level visual navigation, and how to operate in a small cockpit. A student's reactions provided an early indication of whether they were a likely candidate for flying fighter aircraft. The four T-37 fights were followed by a series of flights on the T-43 starting with dead reckoning, getting from point A to point B, then integrated operations, learning to operate the radar at high altitude, and finishing with track selection.

The FAR track was tailored to prepare the navigator for, among other types, the F-15E Strike Eagle as a weapon systems officer (WSO) operating in the aft cockpit. Training included T-43 flights flying from Mather to other bases during which the student gave the headings and made all radio calls, a series of low-level missions, electronic warfare, bombing, and integrated tactical navigation. Finally, students flew another ten T-37 flights, to complete the course. Neil completed his course in 1991.

Discussing the changes made to navigator training since his time, Neil said: "Years later I served as the 479th Flying Training Group commander based at Naval Air Station Pensacola, Florida, home of the combat system officer [CSO] school [the term navigator was replaced by combat systems officer in 2009]. Navigator training moved from Mather to Randolph Air Force Base in San Antonio, Texas for many years [1992-2010] until the US Navy and the US Air Force decided they would train their respective naval flight officers and CSOs together. Operations were stood-up at Pensacola in October 2009, but the air force could not figure out how to train with the navy. So even today, the air force trains its CSOs at Pensacola, but the two services don't train

"The squadron had some Vietnam veterans, and a lot of Desert Storm veterans. At the time the F-15E community comprised an amazing mix of cultures."

AT-38B Talon 65-10450 over the plains of New Mexico during a 479th Tactical Training Wing Lead-In Fighter Training flight near Holloman Air Force Base in 1987. The AT-38B carried external armament and weapons delivery equipment for training. US Air Force/TSgt Jose Lopez

together. The fighter-bomber students fly in the back of a T-6 Texan."

TRIPLE NICKEL

"On completion of the course at Mather I was sent to Holloman Air Force Base, New Mexico for lead in fighter training or LIFT with the 479th Tactical Training Wing, a five-week course. My next station was Luke Air Force Base, Arizona to train as a WSO in the F-15E Strike Eagle with the 555th Fighter Squadron 'Triple Nickel', at the time a component squadron of the 405th Tactical Training Wing.

"The squadron had some Vietnam veterans, and a lot of Desert Storm veterans. At the time the F-15E community comprised an amazing mix of cultures. We had air-to-air expertise from the F-15C community and air-to-ground expertise from the F-4 and F-111 communities. The F-111 guys had a lot of experience of low-level flying and precision-guided munition expertise. We even had close air support and gunnery expertise from the A-10 community. When you put all those different cultures together, it made for an amazing training experience for a young student. I graduated from the second to last class held at Luke in 1992 after which F-15E training was moved to Seymour Johnson Air Force Base, North Carolina."

Discussing his WSO training at Luke, Neil said: "The course was six months long which at the time was run by a wonderful group of instructors, all of whom had different strengths. They all took their jobs seriously, and so they spent a lot of time with us, but they also expected a lot of us. It was an old school approach to learning, where, if you came unprepared, they would not tolerate that at all. After academics, the flying started with a familiarisation phase, then we moved through air-to-air, and finished up with air-to-ground, where you learned how to fly at low altitude, how to work on a controlled air-to-ground range or target range. The course finished with an exercise which involved striking a target within enemy territory against an opposed threat, deep

F-15E Strike Eagle 91-0601/OT assigned to the 422nd Test and Evaluation Squadron takes off at Nellis Air Force Base, Nevada to test the 2,000lb GBU-56C GPS-guided munition. US Air Force/William Lewis

nterdiction style, and return to base without osing anybody.

"Tactics were still very much focused on he former Soviet Union at the time, as you vould imagine, a lot of deep interdictions, nd a lot of learning about the surface-to-air nissile threats and different MiGs and Sukhoi ghters that were going to oppose you. As community, we continued to train to those hreats before things changed after 9/11."

WSO ROLES

Describing how a pilot's and a WSO's role liffered, Neil said: "At the time I started raining, you would hear a common descriptor vhere the pilots would say, I ride the boat, and he WSO shoots the ducks. In the F-4 and in he F-111, the pilot was responsible for flying he jet, and the WSO did everything else. For example, in an air-to-air intercept the WSO vould run the radar at well beyond visual range nd at a certain tactical range would hand over the radar to the pilot, and then monitor he intercept and provide a little guidance on oursuit curves and check six for opposing ighters sneaking up behind us.

"The community followed that method hroughout the 1990s, and I remember distinctly while on the weapons school course in 1997, my pilot, Dave Iverson, who s currently a three-star general and the commander of 7th Air Force in Korea, could operate the sensors in the front seat as good as any WSO could in the back seat. Dave was one of the first guys that ran the radar just he way F-15C and F-22 pilots did. The F-15E community didn't do it that way at the time so naving the pilot run the radar and more of the sensors was a big cultural shift at the time, but t's the norm now.

"When Dave and I went through weapons school in 1997, the F-15E's infrared argeting pod was starting to be used for air-to-air engagements, originally, it was just used as a laser designator for Paveway II weapons. Thanks to a software update we could slave the targeting pod to the radar. As a crew we got good at Dave running the radar and me running the targeting pod, working together as a crew to manually keep track of a lot of different aircraft. Today it's more automated with the ability to slave to Link-16 and other sensors.

> **"Tactics were still very much focused on the former Soviet Union at the time, as you would imagine, a lot of deep interdictions, and a lot of learning about the surface-to-air missile threats."**

"The driver behind that change was efficiency. Every time that you must coordinate something in the cockpit, it's another opportunity for the coordination to break down. Coordination typically requires some sort of inner cockpit communication, yet the level of communication between pilots and WSOs was declining but there was no reason for it to happen the way it was happening. As the E model community began to understand that, and given that the single-seat F-15C and F-16 were doing just fine without a WSO, F-15E pilots were the same such that the question was asked, what is the WSO going to do? As it turned out, there was more than enough for the WSO to do without running sensors that the pilot could run."

Much of the WSO's evolving tasking came from the advent of more and more precision-guided weapons which increased the WSO's workload, as Neil explained: "There were three main categories of weaponry. When I started out, ballistic weapons were still the norm, and they were more of a pilot weapon than a WSO weapon, because the jet had to be flown to a release point, to drop the bomb. Precision-guided munitions brought more requirements for the WSO. You had to find the target in the targeting pod. You had to provide laser energy to guide the bomb. You had to make sure the targeting pod was not masked so the mission planning required you to avoid that, which was intensive. Now, with the advent of GPS-guided weapons, determining what coordinates to put into the weapon is a science, and as each tranche of weapons has become more complex, it has required the WSO to spend a lot more time checking the co-ordinates to make sure the munition hits what it's supposed to hit."

Despite that, the WSO does not have weapon release authority nor is that possible because there is no red pickle button in the aft cockpit. The WSO's role is to get the target designated and get the weapon or weapons ready for release. Explaining the targeting process, Neil said: "You typically fly into a launch acceptable range, dubbed a LAR. Once in the LAR the weapon can be released so the WSO must get everything ready to go, and the pilot consents to release and the weapon comes off when it needs to."

The pilot of an F-15E Strike Eagle assigned to the 335th Fighter Squadron based at Seymour Johnson Air Force Base, North Carolina, prepares to taxi out for a training mission during Exercise Green Flag-West at Nellis Air Force Base, Nevada. US Air Force/Senior Airman Brett Clashman

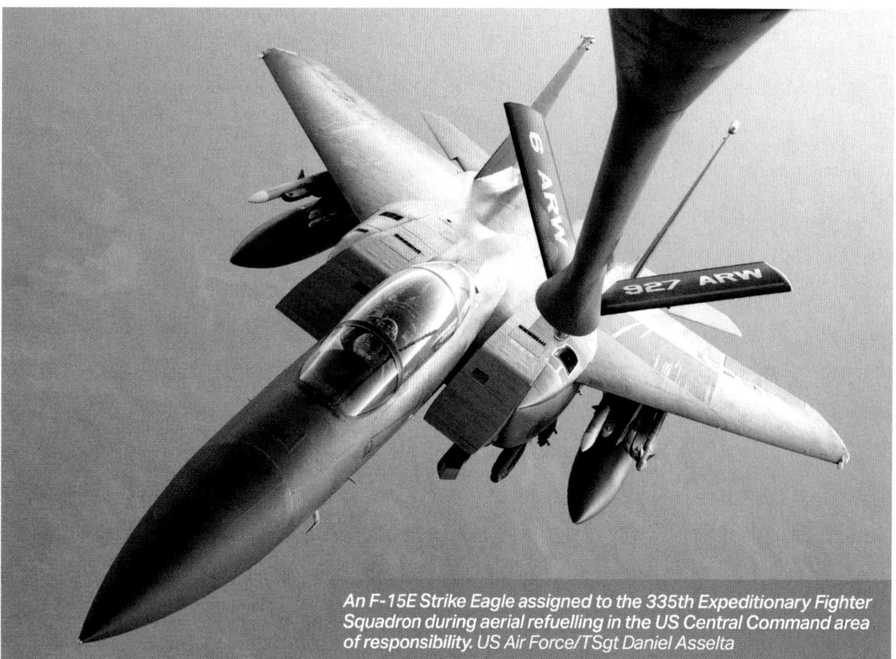
An F-15E Strike Eagle assigned to the 335th Expeditionary Fighter Squadron during aerial refuelling in the US Central Command area of responsibility. US Air Force/TSgt Daniel Asselta

Neil described his performance on the course as average saying he did well in some areas, and not so well in others, "and you probably won't find another flyer that struggled with air sickness more than me. It was awful, but I was very determined that I wanted to fly jets for a living so remained determined to get over it. Things started to improve after I'd achieved combat mission ready status at Lakenheath about a year after I arrived there."

Neil also explained how a student WSO was graded at the end of the course: "Because you're not flying the aircraft, you can't be graded on piloting skills, so you're graded on things likes situational awareness, timeliness, your ability to provide useful information, your ability to think ahead and be prepared for the next phase of the mission. For example, if you're transitioning from a low altitude ingress to a controlled range, are you able to tell the range controller the right things? Your radio and internal cockpit communications are things you're graded on. If your sortie preparation, your ability to mission plan, brief different topics, airmanship, situational awareness, sensor operation, preparations for weapon delivery, laser target designation, striking the target, were good you got a good grade, and if you missed, you got a poor grade - it was straightforward."

JOINING THE LIBERTY WING

After successfully completing his course at Luke, Neil was assigned to the 48th Fighter Wing based at RAF Lakenheath, England in August 1992. He joined the 492nd Fighter Squadron 'Bolars', at the time the only squadron based at Lakenheath operating the F-15E. It was in its transition and had five F-15E aircraft assigned.

Detailing flight operations at Lakenheath, Neil said: "My flying at Lakenheath started with mission qualification training [MQT]. I was crewed with an F-111F pilot who was also flying for his F-15E MQT certification. The MQT course was truncated version of the B course I'd just finished at Luke, but it was operationally focussed and finished with lots of threat-based scenarios. It took four months to complete after which I started nuclear surety certification, run by officers assigned to the 48th Fighter Wing and graded by European Command nuclear surety inspectors.

"Flying in the UK was wonderful. The thing I remember mostly about it was the low altitude flying, I think we were all cleared to fly down to 200. The British low fly structure is better than anything in the world. I also remember the ability for us to engage other

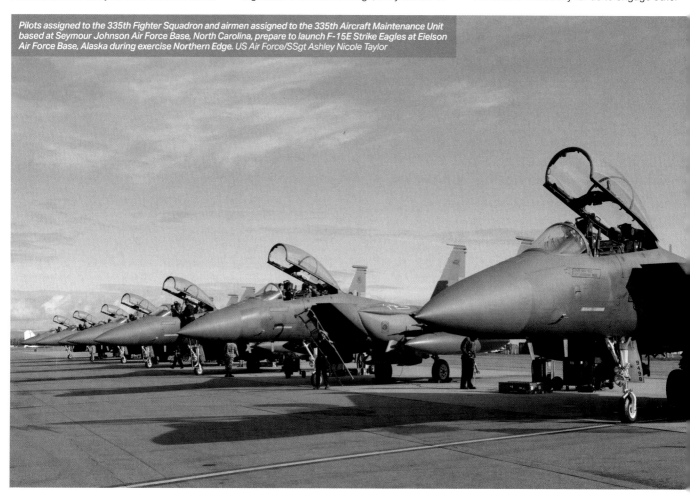

Pilots assigned to the 335th Fighter Squadron and airmen assigned to the 335th Aircraft Maintenance Unit based at Seymour Johnson Air Force Base, North Carolina, prepare to launch F-15E Strike Eagles at Eielson Air Force Base, Alaska during exercise Northern Edge. US Air Force/SSgt Ashley Nicole Taylor

F-15E Strike Eagle 87-0171/LA painted in the markings of the 405th Tactical Training Wing based at Luke Air Force Base, Arizona, the wing that Neil Allen trained with as a student WSO. US Air Force

eroplanes flying at low altitude, it was called ne fighting edge. Squawking a specific code ndicated you were conducting air-to-air ngagements, and we flew around engaging ircraft without communicating with them vhich kept you on alert.

"The east coast ranges weren't too far from ase which allowed us to practice regularly nd in various weather conditions which vas good for training. At the time we were ocused on air-to-ground, influenced by the -111 community co-based at Lakenheath. even out of every ten sorties flown were ir-to-ground and included dropping BDU-33 ractice bombs on the east coast ranges. very now and then we flew to Scotland and it some of the ranges up there.

"Proximity to NATO allies was beneficial. I ot checked out as mission capable ready vith the Bolars and was quickly reassigned to ne 494th Fighter Squadron 'Panthers'. The quadron was invited to be part of the NATO iger community during that time. Even though ve were Panthers, they wanted to have F-15s nvolved. We sent crews to Florennes Air Base, elgium for the NATO Tactical Leadership rogramme which was also extremely eneficial for the crews.

"In 1993 we started rotating in and out of ncirlik Air Base, Turkey as part of Operation rovide Comfort. We logged a lot of hours, vith 50-minute transit times between Incirlik nd northern Iraq, and you would spend a lot f time on a CAP [combat air patrol]. We held nultiple CAPs for most of the day, to ensure aqi aircraft didn't come north of the 36th arallel. That provided a lot of time to practice sing the sensors and learn the jet's systems o a deeper level. The flight hours were logged s combat support time."

In 1995, the 48th Fighter Wing deployed to viano Air Base, Italy in support of Operation eny Flight when he flew missions in the OR in support of the operation. Ironically, IATO's bombing campaign, Operation Deliberate Force started on August 31, the day Neil left Lakenheath for his next assignment with Air Combat Command's 422nd Test and Evaluation Squadron, an operational test unit, based at Nellis Air Force Base, Nevada. He described his second assignment as phenomenal for a young WSO: "I learned so much about weapons employment and dropped every munition that the F-15E could carry.

"The first takeaway from my time serving with the 422nd was realising just how much I didn't know. The experience level in the 422nd was incredible, a lot of senior captains and majors, most of them weapons school graduates. The second was learning about the importance of interoperability, the ability to engage with other communities and their types of aircraft to understand the limitations or strengths of their sensors or their weapons. The third, was realising how immense the Nellis range complex was at the time, millions of acres of unrestricted airspace, all you had to do was stay out of area 51."

> **"When I started out, ballistic weapons were still the norm, and they were more of a pilot weapon than a WSO weapon, because the jet had to be flown to a release point, to drop the bomb."**

F-15E WEAPONS SCHOOL

At the end of his tour with the 422nd, Neil was selected to attend the US Air Force Weapons School. Describing his time at the school, Neil said: "My class comprised two crews but the pilot I was crewed with washed out early in the course which forced me to learn even more, because I had to do everything for the course alone. Given you were supposed to crew coordinate as an as F-15E crew and work together, the instructor pilots that I flew with did just enough for me as a student, but no more. It was a good learning experience but was lonely for sure. Not having a fellow student to bounce my ideas off and help if I didn't get enough sleep the night before was tough, a lot of single seat pilots experience that and I know exactly how they feel.

"So many of the sorties were amazing. The magnitude and the orchestration of the [final] mission employment phase was impressive. On one mission some US Marine Corps F/A-18s based at Miramar provided Red Air for a night-time strike. The instructors required us to cover four different targets in one pass dropping 500lb Paveway II munitions. This forced you into a tactic known as double down, where you would release two weapons, and 30 seconds later, release two more, so all four of your weapons were flying in the air at the same time. You lasered the first two in, changed the laser code and lasered the second two in. It worked well, all four bombs hit where they were supposed to. Back at Nellis, the US Marine Corps Hornet pilots knew we, two F-15Es, had dropped eight bombs but thought there were more aircraft involved. 'Where are the other aeroplanes,' one asked? They were amazed we were able to drop eight in

"The British low fly structure is better than anything in the world. I also remember the ability for us to engage other aeroplanes flying at low altitude, it was called the fighting edge."

F-15E Strike Eagles assigned to the 4th Fighter Wing perform an elephant walk down the runway at Seymour Johnson Air Force Base, North Carolina during a training mission which involved nearly 70 aircraft. US Air Force/SSgt Elizabeth Rissmiller

one night-time mission citing that their squadron had four bombs to drop all year. That was a wake-up call for me, realising how lucky we were that the air force spent money on munitions for us to practice with.

"My three takeaways from the weapons school course are one, instructing done well is hard to do and is truly a profession. For the remainder of my career, I strived to be a great instructor, and it was based on what I learned at weapons school. Second, the three characteristic drivers followed by the today's weapons school are credible, approachable, and humble. In the past, weapons school instructors hammered the students which was meant to make them tough; that was the way it worked. During the time I was there, the weapons school started to change the way it focused on teaching you [the student] as much as possible about your weapon system, the other aircraft around you, and how to be an effective instructor."

Neil graduated from the weapons school in December 1997 and went back to the 422nd TES as a new patch wearer, serving there through the first half of 1998. Surprisingly, Neil disliked his time at the weapons school saying it was hard work, but he learned a lot. In July 1998, Neil was assigned to the 4th Fighter Wing based at Seymour Johnson Air Force Base, North Carolina to serve with the 334th Fighter Squadron 'Eagles'. Explaining his new assignment, Neil said: "The 334th was one of two F-15E Formal Training Units assigned to the 4th Fighter Wing, the other was the 333rd 'Lancers'. I immediately went through an instructor course, which was interesting given my then recent experience at weapons school and started working as an instructor WSO trying to teach guys how to do basic things which was harder than teaching experts how to do other things.

"Typically, an instructor pilot and an instructor WSO flew with a student pilot, and student WSO. The instructor pilot flew the lead aircraft with the student WSO in the backseat,

An F-15E Strike Eagle assigned to the 48th Fighter Wing based at RAF Lakenheath, England. US Air Force/Airman 1st Class Jessi Monte

F-15E Strike Eagle 98-0134/LN assigned to the 492nd Fighter Squadron 'Bolars' launches for a training sortie at RAF Lakenheath, England. US Air Force/Airman 1st Class Jessi Monte

and the student pilot flew the number two aeroplane with me, the instructor WSO, in the backseat. Ninety percent of the sorties were configured that way. So, I spent a lot of time with the pilots flying in the backseat and learned how to effectively instruct them. When they missed radio calls, that typically meant they were task saturated. You could listen to their breathing. From the backseat you can see where their head is pointed, so you know what they're looking at. You just learned how to do these things after you did them enough.

"As the squadron weapons officer, I was also the lead instructor so my job was to make sure that all the instructors were as effective as they could be."

During his time with the 4th Fighter Wing, Neil regularly flew with the 335th Fighter Squadron 'Chiefs' and the 336th Fighter Squadron 'Rocketeers', and the 334th undertook short deployments. Two examples were to Luke to support the F-16 squadrons or to Nellis to support the weapons school or for a flag exercise. These were done to keep the instructors on their game.

Once Neil's tour at Seymour was complete, he returned to Nellis to serve as a weapons school instructor for about three years, finishing in 2003. He then went to the Air Force School at Montgomery Air Force Base, Alabama for two years, then spent a year in the Republic of Korea on the 7th Air Force staff. When he returned from Korea in 2006 with the rank of lieutenant colonel, he returned to Seymour Johnson to serve as an operations officer with the 335th Fighter Squadron, then as the assistant director of operations with the 333rd Fighter Squadron 'Lancers', and ultimately the commander of the 336th Fighter Squadron.

"Because you're not flying the aircraft, you can't be graded on piloting skills, so you're graded on things likes situational awareness."

Explaining his command tour with the Rocketeers, when the squadron deployed to Bagram, Afghanistan in 2009 he said: "The challenge and stress came from providing 24/7 coverage by flying four to four-and-a-half hour sorties. There were always F-15Es airborne, sometimes two, sometimes four. You were either looking at something of interest or in an area where the ground commanders felt like things would heat up, when you were often called to a troop in contact. At the time, the commander was focused on de-escalating the war in Afghanistan, winning hearts and minds was the name of the game, which generally meant you only bombed if it was a last resort. So, we endured a lot of loiter or CAP time but often something would suddenly heat up and you would have to get to the scene quickly and be ready to shoot the gun or drop bombs if need be.

"My command tour ended early in 2010 when I was sent to another school, promoted to a colonel, and became a group commander but didn't fly the F-15 again, but for one time. In 2017, my friend Don Yates, the 48th Operations Group commander at Lakenheath invited me and my other F-15E colleague, who were working in the US Embassy in London at the time, to fly a final flight. That was in June 2017. I retired from the US Air Force later that year."

Eagle Exchange

Royal Air Force officers, Bob Bees, Dave Lewins and Craig Penrice, share their experiences of flying the F-15 Eagle on exchange tours with the USAF.

The military personnel exchange programme commenced in 1971 when the Royal Air Force and US Air Force agreed to allow each other's personnel to fill reciprocal positions. Today, the range of specialisations includes air transport, fast jet, rotary wing and ISR platforms.

In the late 1980s, Bob Bees, Dave Lewins, and Craig Penrice, all qualified weapons instructors, were selected for the F-15 Eagle. Dave was assigned to the 405th Tactical Training Wing based at Luke Air Force Base, Arizona, Bob, and Craig were assigned to the 325th Tactical Training Wing based at Tyndall Air Force Base, Florida. At home, Dave was a Phantom pilot, Bob, and Craig both flew Lightnings.

All three undertook the F-15 transition course to learn the ropes of flying the Eagle, followed by an instructor training course.

LIGHTNINGS AT BINBROOK, EAGLES AT TYNDALL

Craig Penrice left the Lightning-equipped 11 Squadron based at RAF Binbrook, Lincolnshire in November 1987 to join the 325th Tactical Training Wing for a three-year exchange tour where he completed two courses, an F-15 transition course and the F-15 instructor conversion course. Describing the conversion course, Craig said: "You flew one of each type of sortie during which you gave the instruction to an experienced F-15 instructor."

Once he checked out of the conversion course, Craig joined the 95th Tactical Fighter Training Squadron and started instructing students on the F-15 B-course. Speaking about this, Craig said: "As a newly qualified instructor pilot, you were fully fledged and cleared to teach students anything and everything that was on the syllabus. You relied on your instructional experience, common sense, and airmanship to make sure you gave the student the best advice that you could.

"The US Air Force method of instruction was very much brief focussed, in which the instructor described exactly what the student pilot would to see, feel, and hear during the mission to make sure the student was well prepared." Explaining, Craig continued: "You needed to make sure there was no doubt in the student's mind about what the mission was going to be like, what was expected, what it was going to feel like, and what would be considered as good and as bad. You made sure that every aspect of the mission was covered."

One aspect of the exchange tour was to familiarise themselves with US Air Force procedures and culture. Explaining, Craig said: "The RAF trained its pilots to be leaders and able to take over and take charge from the very beginning, whereas the US Air Force system was very much geared to producing wingmen, before upgrading to flight lead roles."

American terminology was another thing that Craig had to become familiar with, as he explained: "It was important for me to recognise that the right words at the right time, held great importance. For example, a pairs take-off is a term used in the RAF that refers to two aeroplanes taking off in close formation, in the US Air Force it's termed a wing take-off."

Describing the F-15 Eagle, Craig said: "It's an awesome aeroplane with a perfect aerodynamic design for the job with a huge cockpit, lots of space, well laid out, and a very capable radar and weapons to match. At the time, Sparrows, Sidewinders, and the M61A1 gun. It had a head up display with an aiming computer that told you where the gun was going to hit. It was a very serviceable aeroplane; rarely did you lose a sortie because the aeroplane was unserviceable. If the radar displayed a fault code at start, you called it in on the radio, a van appeared, and avionics specialists plugged in a computer to identify the issue and swapped out a line-replaceable unit so you could continue with your mission. You also had a dedicated crew chief.

"The F-15 was very honest, you soon felt when it was nearing its limit. A gentle buffet indicated that you would not get the best performance from the aeroplane. You could feel when you were flying at the best performance criteria. If things were working properly, the aircraft had no vices, and when you knew that things weren't working properly it was very forgiving. The F-15 reached

F-15C 83-0020/TY assigned to the 2nd Tactical Fighter Training Squadron over the Gulf of Mexico on a training mission from Tyndall Air Force Base, Florida. US Air Force/TSgt Michael Ammons

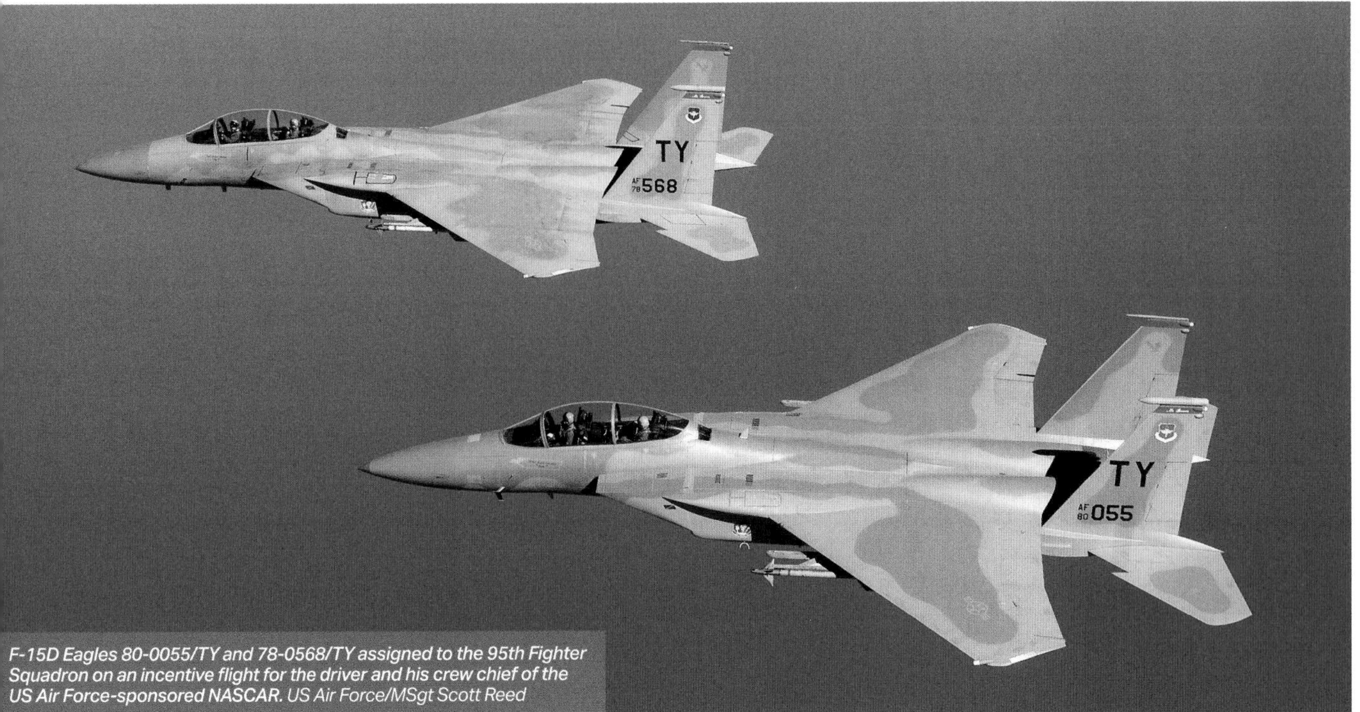

F-15D Eagles 80-0055/TY and 78-0568/TY assigned to the 95th Fighter Squadron on an incentive flight for the driver and his crew chief of the US Air Force-sponsored NASCAR. US Air Force/MSgt Scott Reed

supersonic flight easily, but it took a long time to Mach 2.0 because it was a big aircraft to propel through the air."

AMERICAN ONLY

At the time Craig served as an F-15 instructor pilot, there were several aspects of the aircraft deemed classified and for American eyes only. Providing an example, Craig said: "The situation got to a ridiculous point. Toward the end of the syllabus, we set them a big mission that involved multiple aircraft of different types and told them what the threats were. On one occasion I was the course lead and in charge of the big mission. During my brief to the students, I drew circles on the map to indicate SA-6 and SA-7 surface-to-air missiles. When the students gave their brief on what their plan for the mission was going to be, lots of people attended, including the base intelligence officer. At the point when they unveiled the map, my roughly drawn SAM circles were on there. The base intelligence officer stood up and said, 'you'll have to stop'. 'Why', I asked? 'Because those weapon engagement circles are secret, no foreign'. 'Excuse me, I drew them. They're made up', I replied. 'But it says SA-6 and SA-7, so that makes it secret, no foreign', he retorted. 'But they're not real. They're just for training purposes', I replied. He wasn't having it. And I looked at the boss, and the boss went, sorry, Craig, so I had to leave the briefing!"

While serving with the 95th Tactical Fighter Training Squadron, Craig was fortunate to deploy with the unit to Nellis Air Force Base to participate in Exercise Red Flag with 12 aircraft, but no students. Describing the experience, Craig said: "It was amazing to do that from an American perspective. The dozens of participating aircraft, the threat systems, the build-up, and the execution were great. I'd never been in a big multi-faceted exercise. I flew every other day and managed to avoid Area 51.

The experience of learning how to employ a big strike package rather than just a four-ship was priceless. I lead one mission. Standing in front of an audience comprising dozens of airmen to present my mission plan and how it was going to be executed was daunting, as was the depth of adversaries you were expected to be able to deal with.

"In 1989, the squadron deployed to Roswell in New Mexico to participate in Exercise Roving Sands to provide defensive counter air. This involved night intercepts of B-1B and B-52 bombers tasked to strike targets we were defending against a barrage of electronic counter measures. Despite the electronic threat, rushing over the desert at night, chasing a B-1B was exhilarating.

"On another occasion, we deployed eight aircraft to Naval Air Station Miramar, California for a two-week programme of dissimilar air combat training against F-14 Tomcats. If you did the right things [in an F-15], you should always be able to beat a Tomcat in a dogfight out to beyond visual range. The Tomcat's radar was capable, as were the long-range AIM-54 Phoenix missiles, but those missiles could

"It's an awesome aeroplane with a perfect aerodynamic design for the job with a huge cockpit, lots of space, well laid out, and a very capable radar and weapons to match."

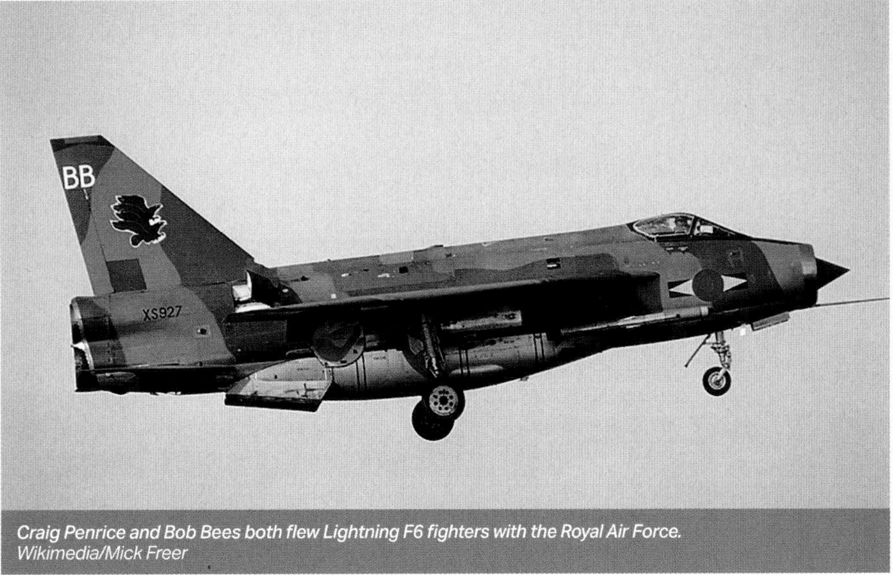

Craig Penrice and Bob Bees both flew Lightning F6 fighters with the Royal Air Force. Wikimedia/Mick Freer

> **"If things were working properly, the aircraft had no vices, and when you knew that things weren't working properly it was very forgiving."**

often be defeated by manoeuvres until you until you got into closer ranges."

When Craig's tour with the 95th Tactical Fighter Training Squadron finished, as a newly promoted squadron leader, he hoped to pick up a flight commander role on a Tornado F3 squadron. Instead, the RAF posted him to RAF Valley, Anglesey to serve as an instructor pilot flying the Hawk T1. After nine months he was selected to attend test pilot school with the US Navy at Naval Air Station Patuxent River in Maryland. Craig was then assigned to MoD Boscombe Down as the first RAF Typhoon test pilot, and subsequently with BAE Systems based at Warton, Lancashire.

LIGHTNING INSTRUCTOR TO EAGLE INSTRUCTOR

Bob Bees arrived at Tyndall toward the end of 1987. He completed three months of transition training with the 2nd Tactical Fighter Training Squadron, then IP conversion with the 95th and then served with the 1st as a newly qualified F-15 instructor pilot.

Describing his initial impressions of the F-15, Bob said: "The power and acceleration of the F-15 were very similar to the Lightning, but it wasn't as slippery as the Lightning. Overall, the F-15 was brilliant to fly, but it did hang on its thrust, so if you came out of afterburner when airborne, you were pulled into your straps, you soon learned to make sure you didn't tighten the straps that well. The visibility was fantastic. If you turned and looked behind, you could see between the tails."

As Bob adopted the American way of instructing, he realised that US Air Force instructors taught students everything from instrument flying to their instrument rating to doing tanking and gunnery. By comparison, in the RAF a qualified flying instructor taught a student how to fly and undertook instrument ratings, before a weapons instructor taught them how to employ the aeroplane as a weapons system, so slightly different.

Discussing his job with the 1st Tactical Fighter Training Squadron, Bob said: "Lieutenant Colonel Richie Smith, who became a two-star general, was my new boss and we were teamed up to do a lot of flying together because he was new to the F-15. He nominated me to become assistant director of operations, third in command with four flight commanders under my watch. I had responsibility for the scheduling and running the flight schedule and making sure we got plenty of days away at weekends to meet the monthly and annual flight hour requirements.

"We flew to Ellington Air National Guard Base, Texas, where the resident 111th Fighter Interceptor Squadron was converting from the F-4D Phantom to the Block 15 F-16A. The squadron wanted us to work with them. Some of the squadron's pilots flew with NASA including the first space shuttle commander who was the general.

"Our big mission plan involved flying combat air patrols and intercepting low-level targets. A KC-135 tanker, led by an RAF exchange officer, was tasked to fly on a tow line that was positioned such that we would not be able to aerial refuel and get to our points for the next CAP timings. We explained the tactical situation to him and asked if he could fly south to meet us. With me leading four F-15s and another RAF pilot leading the tankers, we made the manoeuvre just as we would in the UK, with the tankers flying towards us. During

An F-15D landing at Tyndall Air Force Base. US Air Force/TSgt Demetrius Lester

F-15 Eagles bask in the Florida sunshine prior to launch from Tyndall Air Force Base. US Air Force

the manoeuvre, I told them when to turn so we could run in behind them. We got the first F-15 plugged straight away, followed by the other three, all four aerial refuelling contacts were conducted with a faster fuel flow rate. Everyone involved in the mission thought it was a great manoeuvre, made possible because of the way the two lead RAF pilots had been trained and were allowed to fly the manoeuvre."

When the squadron organised dissimilar air combat training with an F-14 Tomcat squadron, Bob's impression of the cat was a little underwhelming as he explained: "I remember thinking the Tomcat was a fighter that was easy to do combat against because when the wings were extended forward, we could easily exploit that. The F-14's [AIM-54] Phoenix missile was very effective against targets over the sea but performed differently over land because of background clutter in the radar picture.

"By flying tactically and taking head-on shots or by skirting the outside of the Phoenix missile's engagement arc and then entering a 1 v 1 aerial engagement, the F-15 proved superior to the F-14. Once a Tomcat started to slow down and turned to fight you, the wings moved forward. This was our cue to exploit the situation, hopefully scoring a Tomcat kill. That said, the concept of the Eagle was to shoot down aircraft at long range before the adversaries saw you."

Bob flew his last F-15 flight at Tyndall in December 1990 and soon after returned to the UK to serve as the Typhoon Operational Requirements Liaison Officer, the ORLO, based in MoD main building in London. When that assignment ended, Bob served as the BAE

It was a great manoeuvre, made possible because of the way the two lead RAF pilots had been trained and were allowed to fly."

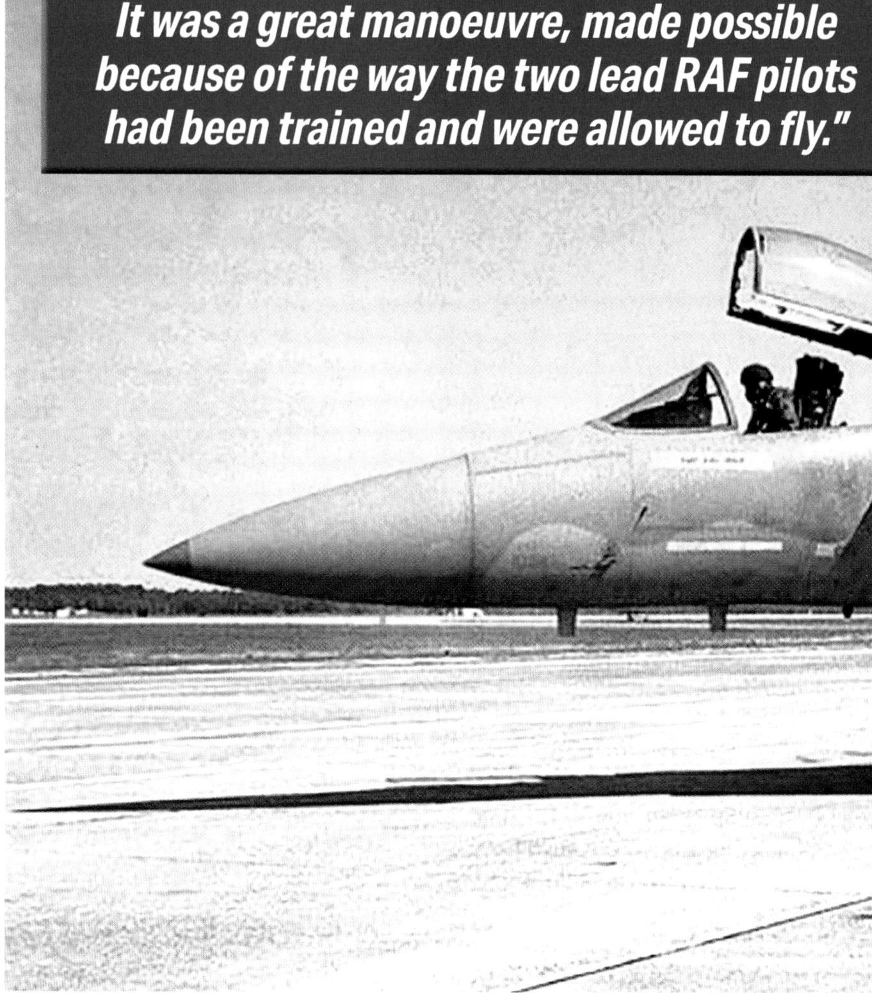

"The visibility was fantastic. If you turned and looked behind, you could see between the tails."

Systems de facto flight operations officer for Eurofighter, and then left the military and joined Virgin Atlantic to fly Boeing 747s.

PHANTOMS AT CONINGSBY, EAGLES AT LUKE

Dave Lewins arrived at Luke Air Force Base as an RAF Phantom-qualified weapons instructor in August 1988 for a three-year assignment.

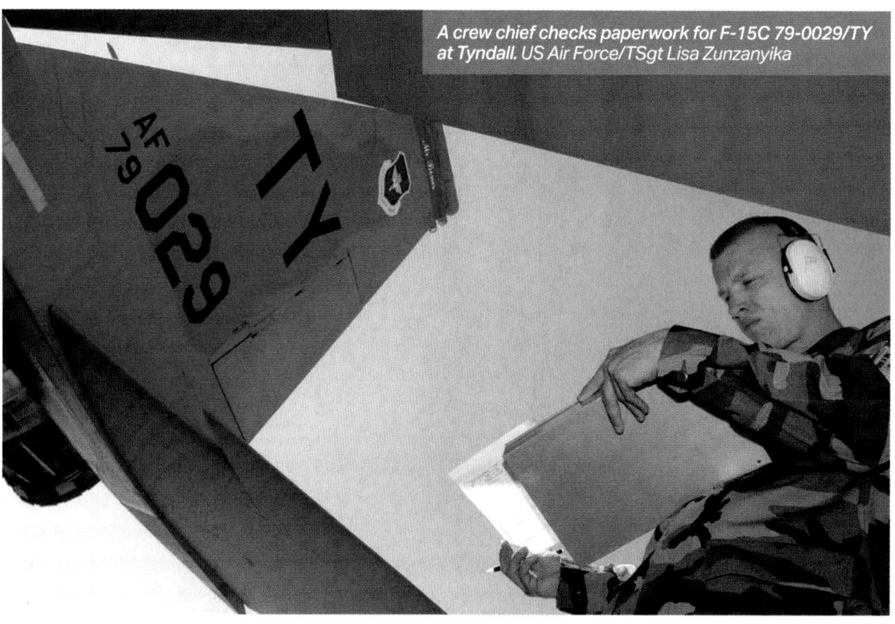

A crew chief checks paperwork for F-15C 79-0029/TY at Tyndall. US Air Force/TSgt Lisa Zunzanyika

Initially, he served with the 426th Tactical Fighter Training Squadron 'Killer Claws' and then due to that squadron's deactivation, he joined the 555th TFTS 'Triple Nickel'.

He soon realised how the American's modu operandi differed considerably to the British. Explaining, he said: "The US Air Force operate with the mentality of large strike packages and taught very different leadership concepts to the those of the RAF. The RAF taught a pilot to quickly lead a two-ship; the US Air Force taught a student to be a wingman for a large part of their early days of training. So, in the second year of an RAF pilot's first tour, they might lead a four-ship, a tactical activity that would take longer in the US Air Force.

"Major Cary Neihans, a very expoerienced instructoir flew me on a staff continuation training sortie between two F-15s and two F-16s. The mission introduced me to high-g, both the F-15 and the F-16 could comfortably sustain 9g, which was phenomenal. The nose authority [the ability to point the aircraft's nose in almost any direction regardless of its track] for example, the roll rate, the pitch rate, the raw power, the radar, and the view were all phenomenal. The radar had lots of features that RAF Phantom FGR2s did not have. The hand controller, for example, in your left hand on the throttles had multiple switches to operate the various radar modes, an action referred to as playing the piccolo.

"Cary allowed me some stick time. You could do pretty much what you liked with the stick, although you could not put it on the

A crew chief talks through the pre-flight checks with the pilot of an F-15C Eagle at Tyndall Air Force, Florida. US Air Force/Lisa Carroll

backstop like you could in the F-16 and F/A-18, because it was essentially a manual control. A beeper sounded at the optimum turn rate and provided an over-g warning if you kept pulling on the stick. You could fly the aircraft on the beeper while looking out and not have to look in at the gauge. Cary told me to pull the stick harder, but when you're pulling 9g for the first time, it's very hard because the forces on the body are crazy. If you were flying at 9g you couldn't really look over your shoulder because you'd hurt your neck. We did neck exercises with weights to help strengthen our neck muscles."

"The RAF taught a pilot to quickly lead a two-ship; the US Air Force taught a student to be a wingman for a large part of their early days of training."

One training event that Dave found staggering was aerial refuelling from a boom, rather than the 'rolling donut' [the drogue on a hose used by RAF tankers]. Explaining, Dave said: "Aerial refuelling from a boom was a lot easier, because you sat in formation behind and under a KC-10 or a KC-135, and the boomer would fly the probe into the receptacle known as a plug. Fortunately, the F-15 was very easy to fly in formation. We flew dual in a two-seat F-15B aircraft on the first tanking mission and solo in an F-15A for the next sortie, underwriting how straightforward the aircraft was to fly at this stage of the course. The same sequence was used for students on the B-course which also involved the first night-time flight to a tanker as a four-ship."

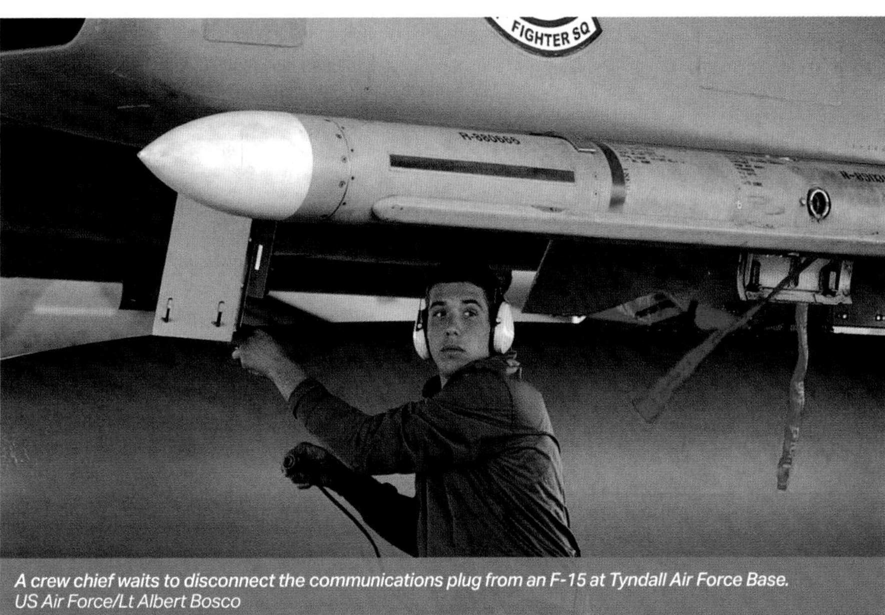

A crew chief waits to disconnect the communications plug from an F-15 at Tyndall Air Force Base. US Air Force/Lt Albert Bosco

Student crew chiefs inspect the rudder and vertical stabiliser of an F-15 as part of their training course at Sheppard Air Force Base, Texas; the same school and course that Brian Maki attended in 1988. US Air Force/Frank Carter

Taking Care of the Jets

Brian Maki served as an F-15 crew chief at Kadena and worked as a maintainer at Langley for over a decade.

Brian Maki was assigned to Sheppard Air Force Base, Texas in 1988 for his technician training course. After completing the course, he was sent to Holloman Air Force Base, New Mexico for further training specific to the F-15 Eagle. At Holloman he attended school for the academic element of F-15 training and worked on F-15 aircraft under the supervision of instructors. Once he was checked out on the F-15 in 1988, he was assigned to the 18th Tactical Fighter Wing at Kadena Air Base, Okinawa where he worked on the flight line for the first time.

Explaining the maintenance organisations at Kadena at the time, Brian said: "Back then the fighter wing had three fighter squadrons assigned: the 12th, 44th, and 67th Tactical Fighter Squadrons, each supported by an Aircraft Maintenance Unit or AMU which were components of the 18th Aircraft Generation Squadron. I was assigned to the

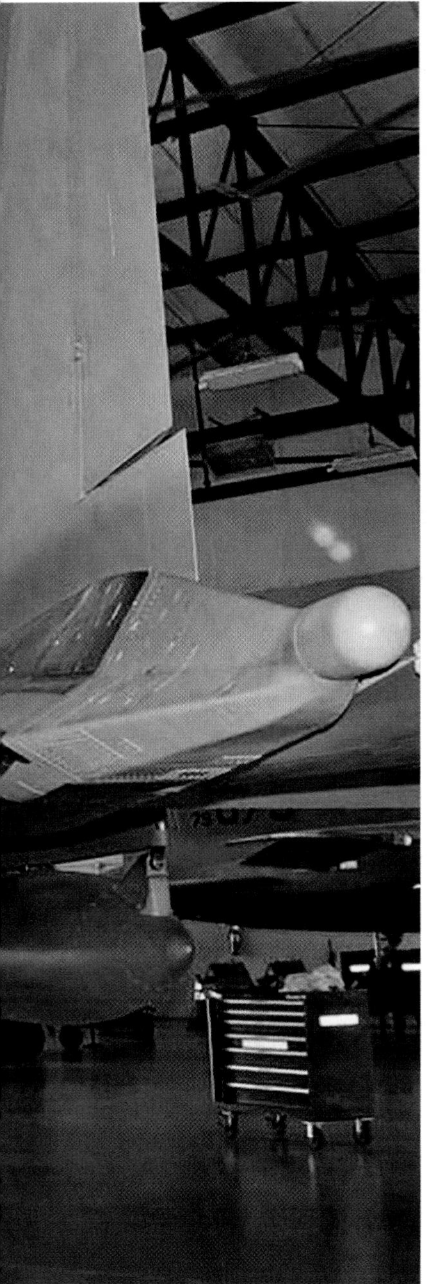

Crew chiefs install a panel on the wing of an F-15. US Air Force/TSgt Scott Stewart

"Toward the end of my tour at Kadena, I was assigned to the phase inspection dock. That was a deeper level of maintenance, when we tore the aircraft apart."

2th AMU as an assistant crew chief. We ʋere known as third wipes; we were the third ssigned to the aeroplane.

"I primarily serviced the aircraft, made ure the oil and hydraulic fluid levels were orrect, serviced the hydraulics, refuelled the ircraft, prepared the aircraft for launch, and onducted all the post-flight servicing. For the ecovery stage you had to record the engine gures by writing them down on a card, figures hat we read from the events history recorder r EHR box and gave those to the pilot to use s part of the debrief.

"Toward the end of my tour at Kadena, I ʋas assigned to the phase inspection dock. hat was a deeper level of maintenance, when ʋe tore the aircraft apart, completed the ıspections and maintenance and then put : back together. On the flight line, the work ʋas more fast paced and more demanding ecause of the nature of flying operations. Vork at the phase dock was more relaxed and ı comparison, the flight line was only more emanding by the depth and thoroughness of he work.

"In 1990, at the end of my Kadena tour, I had orders to the 27th Tactical Fighter Squadron based at Langley Air Force Base, Virginia. The squadron was already deployed to Dharan Air Base in Saudi Arabia for Desert Shield so between October and December 1990 I was assigned to the 94th Tactical Fighter Squadron. Just before Christmas, I was sent to Dharan to join the 27th as part of a maintenance crew that towed and positioned aircraft, serviced, and changed tyres, serviced, and changed the LOX bottles [liquid oxygen bottles]; tasks that relieved the crew chiefs from doing this so-called 'side maintenance'. During my time at Dharan, I didn't work on the aircraft as part of the launch and recovery processes.

"The combat phase, Desert Storm, didn't affect us a whole lot, but when the base was under attack, we had to wear a chem suit, masks, and gloves. The 27th left Dharan in March 1991 and returned to Langley where I was sent back to the 94th. I was happy with that because the 94th is a more famous squadron. During my tour with the 94th I went to engine school under an initiative to include working on engines and hydraulics. We pulled the engines out of the aircraft to change, for example, an air oil cooler. It was reckoned that an engine could be changed in 20 minutes, well it could be if you had all the components set up and ready to go and a complete crew of trained people. Realistically, 20 minutes was not possible."

ENGINE CHANGE

The largest component regularly changed on an aircraft is its engine, detailing the process

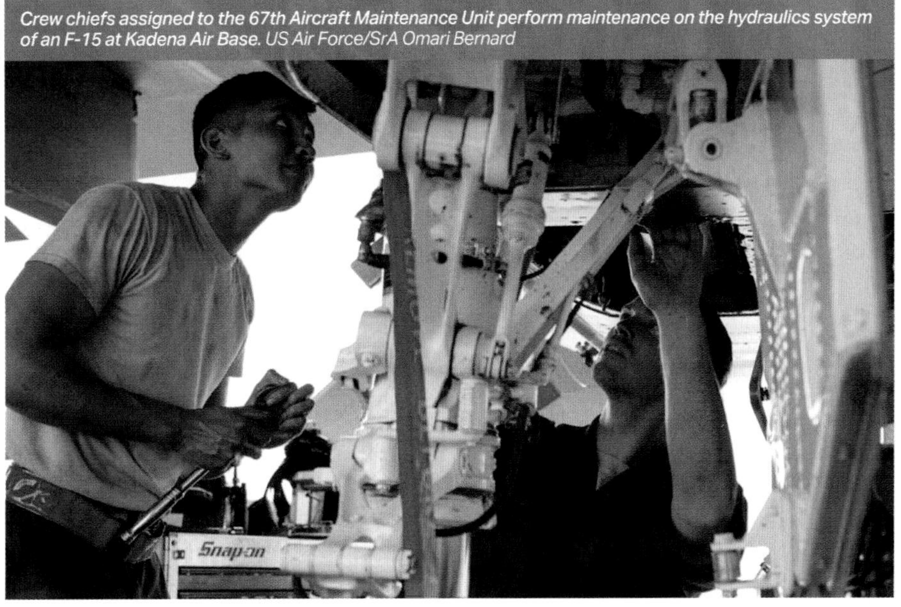

Crew chiefs assigned to the 67th Aircraft Maintenance Unit perform maintenance on the hydraulics system of an F-15 at Kadena Air Base. US Air Force/SrA Omari Bernard

A crew chief assigned to the 67th Aircraft Maintenance Unit changes the oil of an F-15 Eagle at Kadena Air Base, Japan. US Air Force/Senior Airman Omari Bernard

for an F-15, Brian said: "To change an engine, we dropped the underside panels which swung out of the way, then we removed the drop out link which was held in by one bolt. The engine itself had four mounts, two big mounts which we called coke bottles, and two pins less than an inch in diameter, one on the bottom and one on the top in trhe forward position. Each pin had a clamp over the top secured by two bolts tightened by nuts, crimped a little bit at the end so they didn't work loose and spin off. The coke bottles were fitted into the airframe structure by way of the clamps and were chained inside the airframe, so they did not get loose. Two steel rails, one long and one short, which were part of an engine change kit, were positioned, and aligned. Rollers were placed on the rails such that when the coke bottles and fixings were loosened up, they took the weight of the engine and enabled the engine to be pulled straight on to an installation trailer which was linked directly to the rails at the rear. The rails sat on brackets fitted to the airframe, the short rail was on the in board and the long rail was on the out board, and they were pinned in place.

"The engine was disconnected along with the main fuel line, which was about six inches in diameter, to allow the engine to roll out onto the installation trailer. The installation trailer was disconnected from the rails and moved, or it could be connected to a transport trailer which suspended the engine from a cage.

"When an engine had been removed, we inspected it and changed the necessary components such as an air oil cooler or an augmenter fuel pump or wiring. Engines had to be pulled out if the blades had endured foreign object damage and were transferred to the engine shop for a complete tear down and rebuild. As part of the repair procedure, engine specialists' ground and blended the blades leaving a small half-circle where the damaged metal was removed, then covered the repair with blue dye to help preserve the repaired area, which were then re-installed as a perfectly serviceable engine. Once an engine was repaired and rebuilt it was referred to as a pickled engine.

"Once an engine was re-installed, our team had a person who was qualified to run engines on the flight line or on the trim pad when the aircraft was tied down and run up to full afterburner for a functional check and then shutdown. During the engine run, the aircraft was restrained by the tail hook hooked up to a heavy steel bar.

"You ran the engine to max military power ther lit the burner and felt each stage of the burner. That's a real kick in the pants. Interestingly there was no difference in engine rpm between max mil power and afterburner, it's the same rpm, you just put more fuel through the back end with the afterburner engaged, which was graphically shown by the fuel gauge needles! It was always an exciting thing to do.

"The 27th left Dharan in March 1991 and returned to Langley where I was sent back to the 94th. I was happy with that because the 94th is a more famous squadron."

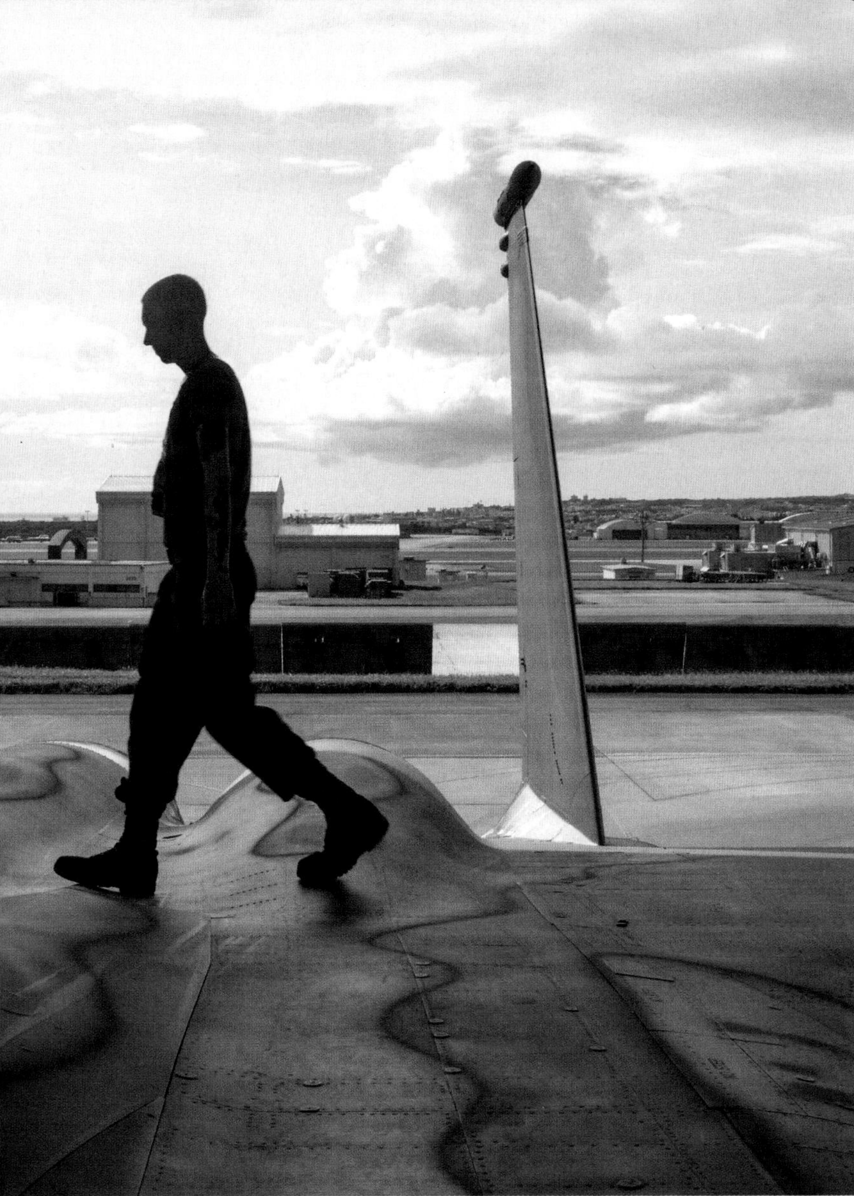

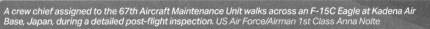

A crew chief assigned to the 67th Aircraft Maintenance Unit walks across an F-15C Eagle at Kadena Air Base, Japan, during a detailed post-flight inspection. US Air Force/Airman 1st Class Anna Nolte

"During my tour with the 94th Tactical Fighter quadron, the squadron deployed to Saudi rabia. On that deployment, a young airman was ying to service the utility system. It takes a lot pumping to get the fluid out of the cart into the eroplane. Apparently, it wasn't going fast enough or him, so he started to tweak the cart until the eroplane pumped the cart full of fluid, which tarved the aircraft's utility system, and pumps of uid, which resulted in the aeroplane's hydraulic ystem getting damaged. I don't know why, but he blame for the incident was pinned on me, esulting in the end of my engine-running career. he flight line guys asked me for a hydraulic art, so I took one out to him and returned to the hop, but I was implicated and got sent back to angley."

ANDING GEAR STRUTS ND CANOPIES

December 1995, Brian transferred to the 1st quipment Maintenance Squadron and worked ith crash recovery, the wheel and tyre shop, nd heavy maintenance which changed large omponents such as the canopy or a landing ear strut. He continued: "Not so much heavy, but tricky, was installation of a hydraulic line through a landing strut up to the top of the wing, which thankfully was rare. I also went different schools to learn about flight controls and rigging."

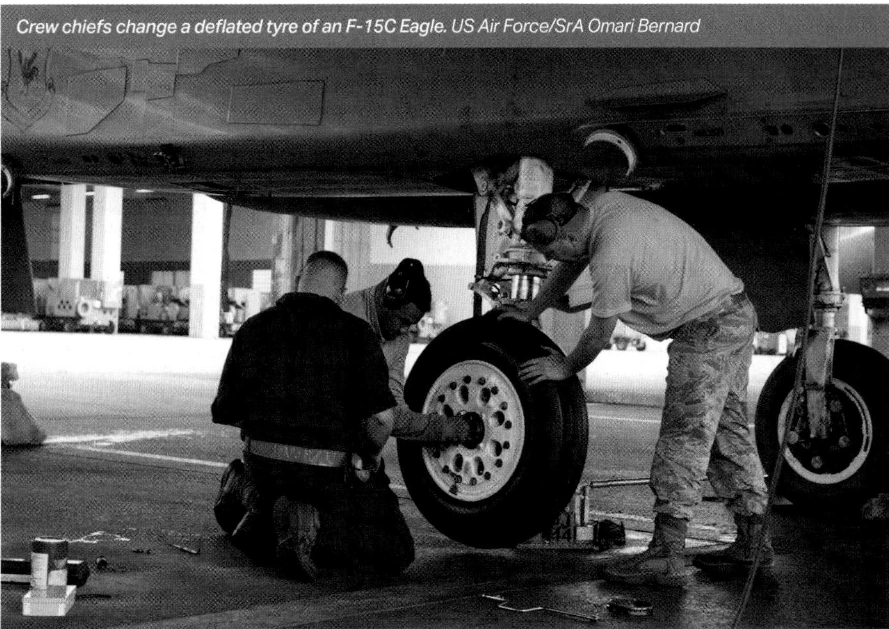

Crew chiefs change a deflated tyre of an F-15C Eagle. US Air Force/SrA Omari Bernard

Discussing different component changes, Brian said: "To change a landing gear strut, we had to jack the aeroplane up, de-service the strut by removing all the nitrogen out of it and hydraulic fluid as much as possible to make it lighter. A main strut took two people to lift, one person could handle the nose strut. Another example was a canopy change. Typically, a canopy would be lifted by crane on to a metal frame to hold it. Canopy removal was only done for specific reasons, most likely seat removal, though that was undertaken by the egress shop. Provided the safety pins were in and none of our team touched anything with black and yellow stripes, which denoted emergency equipment, everything was fine. Before putting a canopy back on the aircraft, it had to be rigged, and which was an involved process. The canopy's fit had to be finely adjusted and sealed off to ensure pressurisation-in-flight without any leaks.

"Anyone involved with rigging a canopy had to attend school to get certified. We used chalk along the windscreen frame to see where the canopy touched the chalk, that way we got a good seal. We had to be careful when fitting a new canopy or landing gear doors, both components had to be rigged to ensure they were closed properly and that all clearances were met. Hydraulic power was put on the aircraft and the strut was retracted slowly to see how the doors closed without impacting anything. It was a very slow process. A more common heavy maintenance action was to remove a rear stabiliser which was a big deal because the component was big. The job involved removing a big actuator which was bolted onto the stabiliser shaft. The stabiliser pulled straight out sideways. The job required a team of four."

At the end of his assignment with the 1st EMS in the spring of 1997, Brian was assigned to the 67th Fighter Squadron based at Kadena for his second tour in Okinawa. This time, Brian worked on the flight line as a crew chief with the E-5 rank which meant his name was applied to the side of his assigned aircraft, F-15C 78-0532. This was Brian's final tour and when his assignment finished, he left the US Air Force.

Eagle Keeper

Robert Blackwell went through technician training at Sheppard Air Force Base, Texas and F-15 training at Eglin Air Force Base, Florida.

Robert attended a technical school at Eglin for a three-month course with an assigned instructor that trained him on every aspect of the F-15. The technical school used aircraft that were sponsored by each of the three squadrons assigned to the resident 33rd Tactical Fighter Wing, the 58th, 59th, and 60th Tactical Fighter Squadrons. The aircraft were mission capable and enabled students to train on how to fix maintenance issues.

Robert's first operational assignment was Bitburg Air Base, West Germany where he served as a crew chief with the 53rd Aircraft Maintenance Unit (AMU).

On arrival at the 53rd AMU, Robert was assigned a trainer who supervised, trained, and signed off his work after he'd completed each task. Once his training was complete, Robert was assigned to specific aircraft as a crew chief with responsibility for inspecting and preparing the aircraft for each mission, for launching and recovering the aircraft, and fixing anything required.

Explaining the role, Robert said: "The crew chief coordinated all maintenance on the aeroplane as performed by the different specialist shops, hydraulics, electrics, machin shop and radar are some examples. I went through a lot of specialised training and was cross trained in all aspects of each system in the jet, so I could work on the jet myself and not have to worry about calling a specialist to complete work."

TIGER MAINTENANCE

The 53rd AMU provided maintenance for the 53rd Tactical Fighter Squadron 'Tigers', one of the three squadrons assigned to the 36th Tactical Fighter Wing based at Bitburg. The Tigers, like its two sister squadrons, was

An AIM-7 Sparrow missile immediately after launch from 48th Fighter Interceptor Squadron F-15A Eagle 76-0118. US Air Force

usy unit that made temporary duty (TDY) eployments to locations around the European ıeatre, which included Aalborg, Denmark, viano, Italy, Decimomannu, Sardinia, and odø, Norway.

Robert recalled a TDY to Bodø in the winter ıonths of January and February working in onditions as low as -65°F (-54°C): "We spent lot of time trying to keep the tyres from eezing to the tarmac, we had to move the ts back and forth. We had to heat up the jets get them to start and wear specific cold eather equipment."

When the US government made the ecision to strike targets in Libya under Operation El Dorado Canyon in 1986, the 53rd Tactical Fighter Squadron was at Decimomannu, Sardinia, a location with less inclement weather than Bodø. The squadron was deployed in a support role to fly combat air patrols and keep the skies clear of any Libyan aircraft. Explaining, Robert said: "Our F-15s were loaded with live missiles and the maintainers were issued with M16 rifles to stand guard of the jets which were ready to launch."

> "We spent a lot of time trying to keep the tyres from freezing to the tarmac."

At Bitburg, the three resident squadrons took it in turn to stand alert. Four mission capable F-15s loaded with live missiles were held on alert, each aircraft housed in an alert barn. Robert was assigned periodically to alert duty. Explaining the alert, he said: "We held 24-hour shifts, we slept and lived there. If the klaxon sounded, the pilots and crew chiefs would run to the aircraft. The crew chiefs helped get the aircraft started and launched within three minutes. The alert was held to

F-15A Eagles 77-0118 (nearest camera) and 76-0090 assigned to the 48th Fighter Interceptor Squadron during North American Aerospace Defense Command's Exercise Amalgam Chief 1987-1 which tested the command's ability to intercept Soviet cruise missiles and aircraft in an attack on North America. US Air Force/TSgt Lou Hernandez

allow F-15s to launch against any kind of Soviet aircraft flying along the border.

"My job and philosophy as a crew chief was to keep the aircraft in a tip top condition so that that pilot could do his job, and nothing would prevent that. Every two or three hours, I walked around my assigned aircraft just to ensure there were no leaks and that nothing appeared to be out of place.

"When an aircraft was on alert, our working practices throughout a 24-hour alert shift were different from the normal practices. If something appeared to be wrong with the aircraft, you could not touch it, you had to notify the maintenance chief right away. He pulled that jet down off alert status, and had a spare aircraft put on alert. You couldn't just open a panel because if a panel was open when the klaxon sounded, you were in trouble. Also, the aircraft was armed with live AIM-9 Sidewinder and AIM-7 Sparrow missiles in a status we called 'cocked and ready to go' so you didn't want to cause a stray spark from scraping your feet on the ground which could cause a missile to fire off or cause a malfunction.

"Whenever the aircraft was in an alert barn, you walk around the aircraft occasionally, looked at it, but you wouldn't go up to it and touch it because it was all tucked in ready. By contrast, whenever an aircraft was in a hardened aircraft shelter and not on alert you could do whatever you needed to do. If something was leaking, you popped the panel and fixed it. But you didn't have to get special permission.

"The importance of the alert barn to launch aircraft to deter any kind of aggression was so important that you couldn't just do what you wanted to do. You had to get all kinds of permission to do anything. You always had to let the pilot and the maintenance supervisor know that you were going out into the bay because they were very leery about any kind of sabotage because the alert aircraft's mission was so important.

"At Bitburg, the task was to keep jets fully mission capable to deter any Soviet aggression. At Langley, the task was similar in nature, but our mission was to keep the east coast and Gulf Coast of the United States safe from any kind of Soviet aggression. Anytime the Soviets launched bombers to fly in international airspace but along the US coast on their way to Cuba, our jets would respond. My mission and that of my maintainer colleagues was to keep our aircraft and pilots flying to accomplish that."

During one TDY at Decimomannu Robert got an incentive ride. His pilot was Major Batchelder, they flew with two F-15s against four F-5E aggressors assigned to the 527th Aggressor Squadron based at RAF Alconbury, England. The F-15s flew slick airframes with no external tanks or pylons.

Picking up the story, Robert said: "I was working the squadron commander's jet that day. He came back from a flight and was commenting about how good I was doing. He said, 'have you ever been up in an F-15'? I said, 'no, sir'. I was an airman first class at that point. 'Go over to life support to get fitted with a flight suit, you're going up this afternoon,' he said. I said, 'let me go tell the flight chief'. 'I told you to go get fitted, I'll tell the flight team,' he said. 'Yes sir,' I replied and went to get fitted for the flight.

F-15A 76-0120 assigned to the 48th Fighter Interceptor Squadron seen at Langley Air Force Base, Virginia in the early 1980s. Note the full-colour national insignia (star and bar) and the light blue-grey colour scheme. US Air Force

"The maintainers were issued with M16 rifles to stand guard of the jets which were ready to launch."

"I remember being in the backseat of the
t at the end of the runway. I couldn't really
e anything but the instrument panel, but
y when he pushed the throttles forward the
ont end came down, and I could see as clear
day. 'Are you ready,' he said? I said, 'yes, sir'
d he pushed the throttles into afterburner. I
lt all five stages of the afterburners kicking
. We took off and got about 50 feet off the
ound, hauling down the runway. He said,
ere we go'. And he pulled back on the stick,
d we went from zero to 18,000 feet just like
at. He told me to look back, which I struggled
do because it's very hard, but I managed to
so and saw the runway going away. After
at I didn't do too well in flight and decided my
ace was on the ground. I'm a crew chief. I'm
t a pilot.

"We went to 7.4g. That was something
se. It was an experience that allowed me to
e what the aircraft goes through. Until that
oint, I did not realise how much the airframe
dures while it's flying. The experience
nbedded in my mind that from that point on
id not let a jet go even with a loose screw
a panel on the top, I made sure it was fixed.
was the most interesting thing that ever
appened to me as a kid. The flight wiped me
ut. On the flight back, flying straight and level,
vas so tired, it was brutal. I have total respect
r the pilots."

Robert's work with the 53rd AMU was
cognised by his commanders and during his
al year at Bitburg he was tasked to train new
chnicians joining the unit how to work on and
rvice an aircraft.

8TH FIGHTER INTERCEPTOR QUADRON

obert completed his tour with the 53rd AMU
Bitburg in 1986. His next assignment was
th the 48th Fighter Interceptor Squadron
ased at Langley Air Force Base, Virginia, the
nly active-duty air defence unit in the United
ates at the time. He described the squadron
one of the best places he ever worked. In
988 he won maintenance professional of the year for the 48th Fighter Interceptor Squadron. He was qualified to perform engine runs which allowed him to start the aircraft's engines and run engine and engine system checks. While working a weekend shift, a US Marine Corps F/A-18 Hornet landed at Langley and parked on the visiting aircraft flight line. Transient alert was not available that weekend, so base ops contacted the 48th Fighter Interceptor Squadron where Robert was at work. An agreement was reached to tow the Hornet to the squadron's area where Robert diagnosed the problem as a hydraulic system leak. He was able to repair the leak which allowed the Hornet pilot to return to his home station, an example of his ability to fix a fighter aircraft's maintenance issue.

F-15A 76-0115/LY assigned to the 48th Fighter Interceptor Squadron shadows a Soviet Air Force Tu-95 Bear bomber during an intercept over the western Atlantic. North American Aerospace Defense Command

> **"If something appeared to be wrong with the aircraft, you could not touch it, you had to notify the maintenance chief right away."**

Robert's assigned aircraft with the 48th FIS was F-15A 76-088 and his pilot was Lieutenant Colonel William Lay who loved the cleanliness and near permanent code one status of the jet. According to Robert, he was one of the few 48th Fighter Interceptor Squadron crew chiefs who was able to maintain a jet with no 'K write ups', issues that aren't pertinent to the jet flying, but need to be fixed later. It was the only jet in the fleet that had no K write ups whatsoever.

While Robert served with the 48th Fighter Interceptor Squadron at Langley the squadron deployed to Nellis Air Force Base to participate in Exercise Red Flag. His big recollection of the exercise was the change in the operational tempo of flight operations compared to the squadron's flight schedule at Langley.

On another occasion the squadron deployed to the Arctic region of Canada in the winter for a two-week period of regional flying for North American Aerospace Defense Command. Recalling the TDY, Robert said: "The sole purpose of the TDY was to train our pilots to fly the mission in the austere environment of the region of Canada where the pilot has very little visual identification and reference when airborne. In wartime, we could be deployed anywhere, whether it be the desert, or whether it be the Arctic, so we had to be ready to deploy to either environment."

Robert left the US Air Force at Langley in September 1989, moved to Orlando, Florida and joined the Florida Highway Patrol as a state trooper.

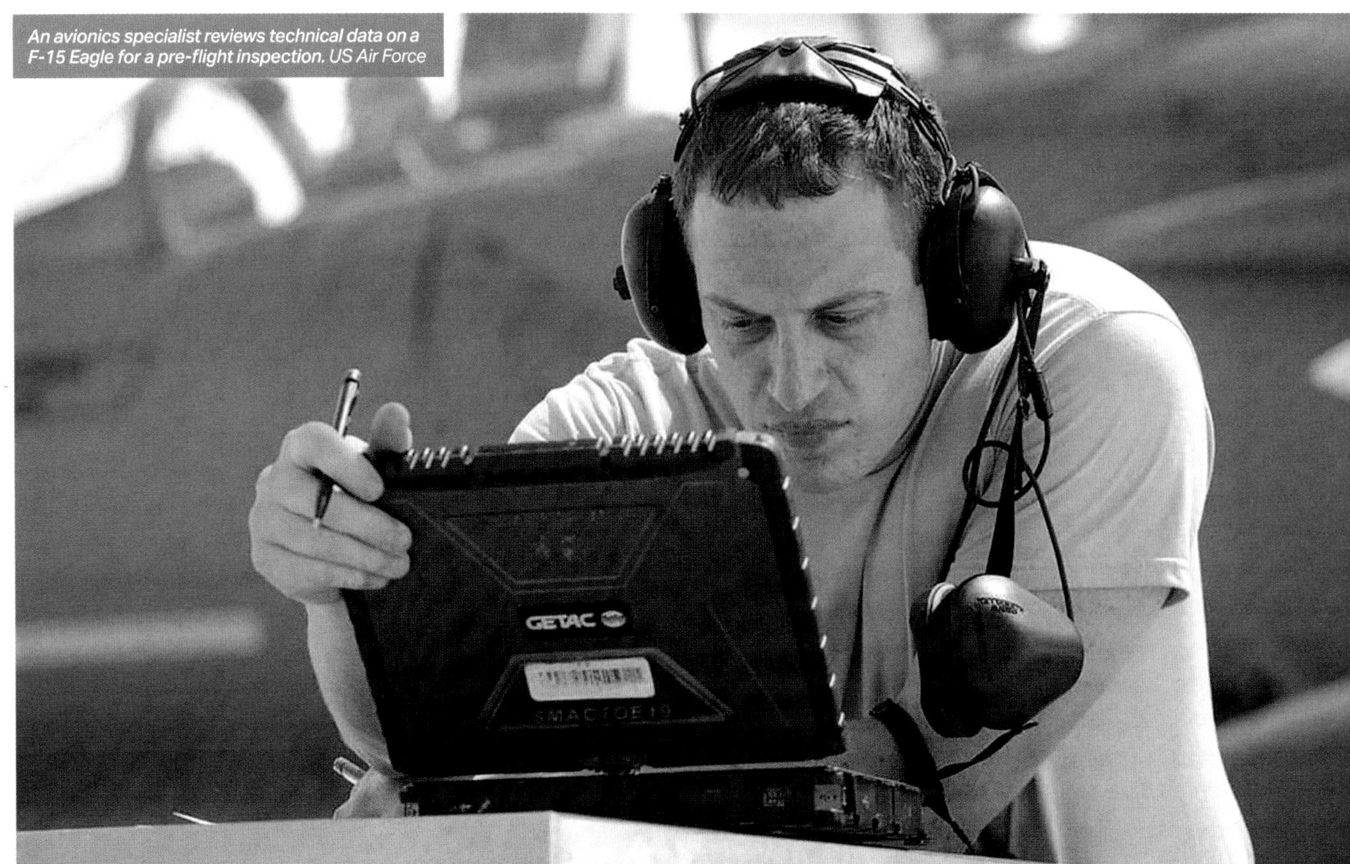

An avionics specialist reviews technical data on a F-15 Eagle for a pre-flight inspection. US Air Force

Avionics Specialist

After completing technical training at the now closed Lowry Air Force Base in Colorado, William Van Kirk served with F-15 units as an avionics specialist.

Unlike a crew chief, an avionics specialist is not assigned to a specific aeroplane but instead works on any that requires rectification of an issue with its radar, guidance system or flight controls.

Discussing his job, William Van Kirk said: "The F-15 is a heavy-avionics aircraft. When an aircraft had an avionics problem, you went to the aircraft out on the flight line to troubleshoot. When an aircraft was in phase maintenance, you followed the avionics-specific work cards. Everything had to be checked before the aircraft rolled out of phase. If the phase crew found something that was an issue, for example a problem with wiring, you had to fix that."

"Air force specialists figured the weight of the gun was causing the aircraft to roll to the right at low airspeed and high angles of attack."

Avionics technicians check the flight controls of an F-15 Eagle at Kadena Air Base, Japan. US Air Force/SrA Lynette Rolen

Detailing some of the F-15 systems aintained by avionics specialists, William aid there were many, which included: "The dar, the EGI which is an inertial navigation nit tied to a GPS receiver, cockpit displays, ie head-up display, the pitot static system omprising a pitot tube, a static port, and itot–static instruments, which determines rspeed and altitude, air data computers, ght controls, the F-15E Strike Eagle has blended system comprising manual flight ontrols and automatic controls, the joint elmet mounted cueing system and electronic arfare systems, primarily the radar warning ceiver, internal countermeasure sets, ountermeasures dispensers, the chaff and are dispensers."

When William started his training, the ionics career field was split into three different sections - attack control, comnav, instruments and flight controls. Explaining he said: "Initially, I worked on instruments and flight controls, which meant I had to know a lot about the whole aeroplane. As you gained more experience, you had to know about everything avionics wise, but you also had to know about flight controls, hydraulics, and engine instruments for which we had to know about the engines. You had to know a lot about the aircraft's systems other than the avionics.

"With enough rank and experience you attended what we called three appeal training detachment, a small training unit that provided specific continuation training. The parent unit was based at Sheppard but ran a detachment at each main F-15 base, I completed my course at Tyndall Air Force Base, Florida, which was my first duty station.

"One issue that regularly popped up with the F-15, which was inherent to the airframe, was a tendency for the aircraft to roll to the right regardless of the pilot's input, specifically at low airspeed and high angles of attack. This was a departure from normal flight and when it occurred, the aircraft was impounded. Only a select group of people were allowed to then work on that aeroplane. A team was hand-

An avionics specialist works on the radar of an F-15 Eagle at Nellis Air Force Base, Nevada. US Air Force/SrA Brett Clashman

picked, and each member had to hold the utmost qualifications. The team had to figure out what the issue was and what the cause was.

"The F-15's M61A1 gatling gun is housed in the right-wing root. It weighs about 250lb, the feed system and ammo weigh another 850lb which is extra weight on the right side only. Air force specialists figured the weight of the gun was causing the aircraft to roll to the right at low airspeed and high angles of attack. At Tyndall in particular, an F-15 training base, student pilots often flew the aeroplane into a position they should not have done. This was countered by providing additional academic instruction to try to ensure student pilots would not fly the aircraft into the situation. The F-15C aircraft's flight controls were rigged to counteract the roll tendency. In comparison, the F-15E and the F-15EX feature advanced fly-by-wire systems that enable the flight control computers to be re-programmed and counteract the effect. During my time at Tyndall, I qualified to be part of the rectification team and had to troubleshoot aircraft flight controls on those occasions when the specific aircraft had been flown into the position that caused the aircraft to roll to the right."

"I learnt on the job, it wasn't super difficult to do the transition that way, but it was hard because I had to complete my academic study in my own time."

At the end of his three-year tour at Tyndall, William was assigned to the 48th Fighter Wing based at RAF Lakenheath in England. This presented a change because he was assigned to the F-15E-equipped 492nd Fighter Squadron 'Bolars' on a four-year tour.

Discussing his new assignment and the transition to the F-15E, William said: "I was supposed to return to school to learn about the F-15E, but as things turned out, I learnt on the job, it wasn't super difficult to do the transition that way, but it was hard because I had to complete my academic study in my own time, which was augmented by a lot of hands on training too. One advantage at the time was that most of the aeroplanes assigned to the 492nd were nearly new, which meant they didn't have a whole lot of issues. My transition to the F-15E at Lakenheath was in the early 2000s, when the wing took delivery of the last new F-15E aircraft built."

Squadrons assigned to the 48th Fighter Wing are constantly busy and spend a lot of time deployed to locations around Europe, in addition to rotations to the US Central Command theatre and regular training deployments to the United States for Exercises Red Flag and Green Flag at Nellis, and for Air Combat Command's Weapons System Evaluation Program held at either Hill or Tyndall Air Force Bases. One regular tasking during William's Lakenheath assignment was Operation Northern Watch to enforce the no-fly zone over northern Iraq. Each deployment was made to Incirlik Air Base, Turkey.

On September 12, 2000, at the end of a transatlantic flight from Langley Air Force Base, Virginia, the last aircraft to land at Lakenheath, F-15E 96-0203, suffered a landing gear failure. William explained the incident: "The left gear didn't turn over. When the gear drops, it's supposed to jerry link over and runaway. On this occasion without the turnover, the tyre

"The aircraft then cartwheeled down the runway until it broke apart."

was facing the wrong way, it was 180 degrees opposite of what it was supposed to be.

"The pilot landed the aircraft, but the tyre blew right away, and the main left gear strut failed because of its perpendicular orientation to the aircraft flight path after gear extension. The aircraft immediately steered to left, departed the runway, caught the barrier, which ended up digging the nose into the ground. Th aircraft then cartwheeled down the runway unt it broke apart at splice point 815, the point on the aircraft where it's supposed to break apart The pilot and weapons system officer did not eject but were removed from the aircraft by tw security forces airmen and three maintainers."

Due to severe damage, the airframe was written off and transferred to the United States, where it was rebuilt in Boeing's Logistics Support Systems facility at Phoenix-Mesa Gateway Airport, Arizona in 2003-2005. The airframe fuselage was matec with a converted F-15B nose section and the whole (non-flying) aircraft now serves as an armament load trainer (designation TFE-24) a Sheppard Air Force Base, Texas.

Picking up the story, William said: "I was one of the last people to work on that aeroplane before it took-off from Langley for the transatlantic flight to Lakenheath. The Langley cops picked us up and took us to the hospital where we had to give blood and pee in a bottle for tests to make sure that none of us had been compromised in any way by the effects of drugs or alcohol. Then the acciden investigators worked through who touched th aircraft, what they did, what happened, to try determine if the incident was caused through maintenance issue or an aircrew issue? I wasr part of the investigation, but they asked me a lot of questions, but we knew right away that i wasn't anything that we had done that causec the incident. The investigation determined the incident was caused by a faulty jerry link switch caused by a design flaw."

At the end of his Lakenheath tour, William was assigned to Sheppard to serve as an avionics instructor for three and a half years, then he went to Maxwell Air Force Base in Alabama to work in the development of training, after which he retired from the US Air Force.

Avionics technicians are responsible for keeping an aircraft's avionics systems operating properly. This photograph shows two avionics specialists conducting avionics system checks out on the flight line at Kadena Air Base, Japan. US Air Force/SrA Lynette Rolen

"We knew right away that it wasn't anything that we had done that caused the incident."